POWER IN PRAISE

by
Merlin R. Carothers

Edited by
Jorunn Oftedal Ricketts

Logos International
Plainfield, N.J.

Unless otherwise identified, all scripture references are taken from *The Living Bible* translated by Ken Taylor, © Tyndale House, Wheaton, Illinois, 1971.

SBN: 912106-25-5
Library of Congress Catalog Card Number: 70–182035
© 1972 by Logos, International, Plainfield, N. J. 07060
Printed in the United States of America

CONTENTS

"If anyone could tell you the shortest, surest way to all happiness and perfection, he must tell you to make it a rule to yourself to thank and praise God for everything that happens to you. For it is certain that whatever seeming calamity happens to you, if you thank and praise God for it, you turn it into a blessing . . . ."

—William Law, English clergyman, eighteenth century

"I thank God for my handicaps, for through them I have found myself, my work and my God."

—Helen Keller

"Blessed is he who submits to the will of God; he can never be unhappy. Men may deal with him as they will . . . he is without care; he knows that 'all things work together for good to them that love God, to them who are called according to His purpose.' "

—Martin Luther

"Cry for grace from God to be able to see God's hand in every trial, and then for grace . . . to submit at once to it. Not only to submit, but to acquiesce, and to rejoice in it . . . I think there is generally an end to troubles when we get to that."

—Charles H. Spurgeon

1

The Power in Praise

Jim's father had been an alcoholic for thirty years. All those years Jim's mother, and later Jim and his young wife, had prayed that God would heal him, but with no apparent result. Jim's father refused to admit that he had a problem with alcohol, and stalked out in anger if anyone ever mentioned religion to him.

One day Jim heard me speak about the power that is released when we begin to praise God *for* everything in our lives instead of pleading with Him to change the circumstances that hurt us.

Jim brought home a tape of the meeting and played it over and over again for his friends. Then one day it struck him; he had never tried praising God *for* his father's condition. Excitedly he shared the thought with his wife.

"Honey, let us thank God for Dad's alcoholism and praise Him that the condition is part of His wonderful plan for Dad's life!"

For the rest of that day they gave thanks and praised God for every aspect of the situation, and by evening they felt a new sense of excitement and expectation.

The next day the parents came over for the usual Sunday dinner visit. Always before, Jim's father had cut the visit as short as possible, leaving right after dinner. This time, over a cup of coffee, he suddenly asked a pointed question.

"What do you think about this Jesus Revolution?" He turned to Jim. "I saw something about it on the news last night. Is it just a fad, or is something happening to those kids who were hung up on drugs?"

The question led to a lengthy and open discussion about Christianity. The elder couple didn't leave till late in the evening.

Within weeks Jim's father came to admit his drinking problem, turned for help to Jesus Christ, and was completely healed. He now joins the rest of the family in telling others what praising God can do!

"Just think," Jim said to me. "For thirty years we prayed for God to change Dad. We spent only one day praising Him for the situation and look what happened!"

The phrases "Praise the Lord!" or "Thank God!" are used so glibly by many of us that we tend to lose sight of their real meaning.

Praise, according to Webster's dictionary, means to extol, laud, honor, acclaim, express approval. To praise, then, is to give positive affirmation, expressing our approval of something. Giving our approval means that we accept or agree with what we approve of. So to praise God *for* a difficult situation, a sickness or disaster, means literally that we accept and approve of its happening, as part of God's plan for our lives.

We can't really praise God without being thankful for the thing we are praising Him for. And we can't really be thankful without being happy about whatever we're thankful for. Praising, then, involves both gratitude and joy.

The very fact that we praise *God* and not some unknown fate also means that we are accepting the fact that God is responsible for what is happening. Otherwise it would make little sense thanking *Him* for it.

"Always be joyful. Always keep on praying. No matter what happens, always be thankful, for this is God's will for you who belong to Christ Jesus" (I Thess. 5:16-18).

I've met many people who are able to praise God for their circumstances, simply because they accept the word of the Bible that they are supposed to praise God in everything. Praising Him, they soon experience the results of an attitude of consistent thanksgiving and joy; and in turn, their faith is strengthened, and they can continue to live this way.

Others find it a little more difficult.

"I just don't understand," they say. "I try praising God, but it is so hard for me to believe that He really has a hand in all the horrible things that have happened to me lately."

We say we don't understand, and some of us get stuck right there; our understanding becomes a real stumbling block in our relationship with God. But God has a perfect plan for our understanding, and when we use it His way, it isn't a stumbling block, but a wonderful aid to our faith.

"For God is the King of all the earth," said the psalmist. "Sing praises in a skillful psalm and with *understanding*" (Psa. 47:7 *Amplified Bible*).

We're not supposed to push our understanding out of the way, grit our teeth, and say, "It doesn't make sense to me, but I'll praise the Lord if it kills me, if that's the only way I can get out of this mess!"

That's not praising, that's manipulating. We've all tried to manipulate God, and it is wonderful to know that He loves us too much to let us get away with it! We are to praise God *with* our understanding, not in spite of it.

Our understanding gets us into trouble when we try to figure out *why* and *how* God brings certain circumstances into our lives. We can never understand *why* and *how* God does something, but He wants us to accept with our understanding *that* He does it. This is the basis for our praise. God wants us to understand *that* He loves us and *that* He has a plan for us.

"And we know that all that happens to us is working for our good if we love God and are fitting into his plans" (Rom. 8:28).

Are you surrounded by difficult circumstances right now? Have you been struggling to understand why they have come to you? Then try to accept with your understanding that God does love you and has allowed those circumstances because He knows they are good for you. Praise Him for what He has brought into your life; do it deliberately and with your understanding.

One couple heard me speak on praising God for everything and went home quite disturbed. For months they had grieved over the condition of their daughter who had been committed to a mental institution and had been diagnosed hopelessly insane.

Prayer groups across the country had been asked to intercede for her, and daily the parents had pleaded with God on their knees to heal their daughter. Her condition remained unchanged.

Their initial response to the challenge that they were praising God *for* the condition of their daughter had left them distraught and unhappy.

"It would be blasphemy," said the wife, "thanking God for something so obviously evil. If we thank Him, doesn't that mean we accuse Him of deliberately hurting our daughter? It just doesn't fit in with my idea of a loving God."

"It doesn't *seem* right," the husband agreed. "But what if that speaker *is* right?"

The wife looked helplessly at her husband.

"I just don't know," she said.

"We have nothing to lose, do we?" The husband looked thoughtful. "Why don't we try it?"

They knelt together.

"Dear God," the husband began, "we know that you love us and that you love our daughter even more than we do. We're going to trust

3

that you're working out in her life what you know is best for her; so we thank you for her sickness, thank you that she's in the hospital, thank you for the doctors who haven't found a way to help her. We praise you God for your wisdom and love toward us . . ."

The longer they prayed that day, the more they became convinced that God was indeed doing what was best.

The next morning the hospital psychiatrist called.

"Sir, there's been a remarkable change in your daughter," he said. "I suggest you come and see her."

Within two weeks she was released from the hospital.

A year later a young man came up to me after a meeting. He introduced himself as the girl's brother and told me that she was married, expecting a baby, and "is the happiest girl in the world!"

A mother came and wanted prayer for her daughter who was a go-go dancer in a nightclub. I told her I would be glad to pray with her and thank God for her daughter's situation. She looked at me in horror.

"Don't tell me I'm supposed to thank God that my daughter mocks common decency and laughs at religion. Surely I've got the devil to thank for her misery, not a loving God!"

The mother was faced with a difficult choice. All her life she had been conditioned to thank God for everything good and blame the devil for everything bad. Together we searched the pages of my Bible for verses stating that God is able to work all things for good for those who love and trust Him, and that He wants us to be thankful in everything, regardless of how evil our situation appears.

"You can go on thinking that your daughter's situation is controlled by the devil—and by your lack of faith in God's supreme power make it difficult for Him to work out His perfect plan for her, or you can believe that God is at work, thank Him for everything and thereby release His power to work in her life."

At last the mother agreed to try.

"I don't understand why it has to be this way," she said, "but I am going to trust that God knows what He's doing, and I'm going to thank Him for it."

We prayed together, and the mother went away with a new peace in her heart about the whole situation.

"For the first time, I'm not worried at all about my daughter," she beamed.

Later she told me what happened.

That same night her daughter was dancing nearly nude on her little platform when a young man came into the nightclub. He walked up to the girl, looked straight at her, and said, "Jesus really loves you!"

The go-go dancer was used to hearing all kinds of remarks from

4

young men, but never anything like this. She came down from her platform, sat down with the young man at a table and asked, "Why did you say that?"

He explained that he happened to be walking down the street when he felt that God was urging him to go into that particular nightclub and tell the go-go dancer that Jesus Christ was offering her the free gift of eternal life.

Stunned, the girl stared at him; then tears filled her eyes, and quietly she said, "I'd like to receive that gift."

And she did, right there at the table in the nightclub.

Praising God is not a patent medicine, a cure-all, or a magic formula for success. It is a way of life that is solidly backed up in God's Word. We praise God, not for the expected results, but for the situation just as it is.

As long as we praise God with an eye secretly looking for the expected results, we're only kidding ourselves, and we can be certain that nothing will happen to change us or our situation.

Praise is based on a total and joyful acceptance of the present as part of God's loving, perfect will for us. Praise is not based on what we think or hope will happen in the future. This is an absolute "law," clearly observable in the practice of praise.

We praise God, not for what we expect will happen in or around us, but we praise Him for what He is and where and how we are *right now!*

It is, of course, a fact that when we honestly praise God, something *does* happen as a result. His power obviously flows into the situation, and we will notice, sooner or later, a change in us or around us. The change may be that we come to experience a real joy and happiness in the midst of what once appeared to be a miserable situation, or the situation may change. But this is a *result* of praise, and must not be the motivation for praise.

Praise is not a bargaining position. We don't say, "I'll praise you so that you can bless me, Lord."

To praise God is to delight ourselves in Him, and the psalmist wrote, "Be delighted with the Lord. Then he will give you all your heart's desires" (Psa. 37:4).

Notice the order of importance here. We don't make a list of our heart's desires and then delight ourselves in the Lord in order to get them. We're first to be delighted, and once we've experienced being really delighted with God, we'll discover that everything else becomes secondary. Still, it is true that God does want to give us all our heart's desires. Nothing short of that is His wish and plan for us.

If we could only learn to be delighted with the Lord in everything first!

A Christian couple had two sons. One was their pride and joy; he lived at home and shared his parents' warm and happy Christian faith.

Once when I was having dinner with them, they confided in me that their older son was a rebel and gone from home. He had graduated from college with honors, but had turned his back on his parents and on established society. Now he roamed the country as a hippie, with no apparent objectives in life.

The unhappy parents asked if I had any advice for them. I explained that I believed that God had given them this son and was answering their prayers for his salvation.

"If your prayers are sincere, then you can be sure that his present life is exactly what God knows is best for him, and for you!" I said.

"I understand," said the father. "We want only what is best for our boy, and this must be God's way and will for all of us."

We joined hands around the dinner table and thanked God for working out His plan in the way He knew was best. Afterward the parents felt a great release and a new peace.

A short time later the family wrote me. Since our meeting, the parents had persisted in thanking God for their son's way of life, even if they found it hard to understand. Then one day their son had an accident on his bike and received a painful injury to his foot.

Temporarily crippled, he decided to come home for a while. He informed his parents that he'd left a trail of unpaid bills across the country. The parents prayed about it and decided that if God had really been at work in all the events in their son's life, He had also allowed the bills. So they thanked Him for every one of them and paid the debts in full!

Their son was amazed. He had expected to be reprimanded and told to take care of his own obligations. Instead, his parents were relaxed, loving, and appeared to accept his way-out style of dress and hair without cringing.

One evening some young Christians came to visit the younger son. The older brother was obviously irritated by the intrusion, but his painful foot kept him from leaving the house. Enthusiastically, the young Christians shared what Jesus Christ had done and was doing in their lives. At first the older brother offered scathing criticism of what he called their naive and unrealistic approach to life, but soon he was listening attentively and asking probing questions. Before the evening was over, he had turned his life over to Jesus Christ.

His parents joyfully wrote that there was an immediate and drastic change in their older son's life. He dedicated himself to follow Jesus and serve Him. Eagerly he studied the Bible, and within a few days he asked for and received the baptism in the Holy Spirit, the experience

6

the followers of Jesus had received on the first Pentecost after Christ's death and resurrection. A few days later he met a Christian girl. Two weeks later they were engaged to be married.

Months of anxious and concerned prayers had not brought a change in this young man. Only when the parents turned to God in joyful acceptance of the present conditions of their son's life was the door opened for God to complete His perfect plan for all of them.

God does have a perfect plan for your life and for mine. We may look at the circumstances surrounding us and think we've been standing still forever in one painful spot. The more we pray and cry for God to help us, the more the circumstances seem to pile up. The turning point cannot come until we begin to praise God *for* our situation instead of crying for Him to take it all away.

A young woman wrote and told me how she had reached the end of her rope. Certain embarrassing personal circumstances had caused her to lose her self-respect, and she began to neglect her looks.

"Eating was my way out," she wrote, "and soon pounds began to pile up all over my body till I looked like a three-ring circus. My husband began looking at other women, and one day he moved out, asking for a divorce."

Bills began to accumulate, her nerves were stretched to the breaking point, and the thought of suicide became more and more frequent.

"All this time I prayed continually," she wrote. "I read my Bible, went to church every time the doors were open, and asked everyone I knew to pray for me. My Christian friends kept telling me to 'keep the faith; don't let it get you down; things will be better tomorrow.' But everything kept getting worse. Then someone gave me *Prison to Praise.* I read it, and at first I couldn't believe you were serious. No one in his right mind could expect me to be thankful for everything that was going on in my life right then! But the longer I read, the more I cried. Slowly it dawned on me that what you said was real. Those scripture verses about thanking God for everything—I'd read them in my Bible countless times and never really understood what they meant."

She decided to try thanking God for everything. After all, what could she lose? She'd been gaining weight so rapidly that she knew she could suffer a serious heart attack at any time. With a faint glimmer of hope she knelt in her living room to pray.

"God, I thank you that my life is just as it is. Every problem I have has been your gift to bring me to the place where I am right now. You wouldn't have permitted any of these things to happen if you hadn't known that it was best for me. God, you really *do* love me! I mean it God, I *know* you do love me . . . "

At this point her prayer was interrupted by the dog barking loudly

7

at the mailman. Every day the dog greeted every visitor to her house with intensive barking; that was one of many irritating little incidents that seemed to pile up to make her days miserable beyond endurance. As she got up and moved toward the door to silence the dog with the usual sharp command, she suddenly remembered, *I'm supposed to be thankful for everything.* "Okay, God, thank you for my barking dog!"

The mailman brought a letter, and she stared at the familiar handwriting on the envelope. It couldn't be! She hadn't heard from her husband for months! God couldn't have moved *that* quickly. With trembling hands she opened the letter and read, "If you are still willing, there may be a way that we can work out our problems."

God's timing had been perfect. Joyfully, this young lady was now able to believe that God was indeed working in her life for good. She went on to lose weight like butter sliding off a hot plate. Her friends began to comment, "You look so good! What has happened to you? You don't look like the same person!"

The same person? Yes and no. She was the same physical being, but she now lived in a new dimension of faith, knowing that God was working in every detail of her life for good. Her husband returned and they were united. She wrote, "Some mornings I wake up hearing myself talking to God, saying things like, 'Oh God, thank you for a beautiful day. I love you!'"

The turning point in her life came when she began to accept her present circumstances with thanksgiving. This is a perfect illustration of the spiritual principle at work.

God has a perfect plan for our lives, but He cannot move us to the next step of His plan until we joyfully accept our present situation as part of that plan. What happens next is God's move, not ours.

Some people would like to deny that fact. They look at the transformation taking place in the lives of people who have learned to praise God for everything, and they insist that the explanation is a simple one.

"A changed attitude brings about changed circumstances," they say. "It is simple psychology. When you stop complaining and start smiling, you feel different; others treat you differently, and your whole life can undergo a dramatic change for the better."

I will agree that the formula, "Smile and the world will smile with you; cry and you cry alone," is a reasonably sound piece of advice—up to a point. But praising God is something more than a change in our own attitude.

There is no power in our words of praise as such. There is no power in our attitude of thankfulness and joy. All the power in the situation comes from God. We need to remind ourselves of that fact frequently. It is easy to fall into the trap of thinking that *we* have the power to manipulate or change a situation simply by reciting a certain form of prayer.

When we sincerely accept and thank God for a situation, believing that He has brought it about, there is released into that situation a supernatural, divine force that brings about changes beyond what can be explained as an unfolding of natural events.

While I was serving as a chaplain at Fort Benning, Georgia, a young soldier brought his wife to my office for help. She was suffering with horrible flashbacks from LSD, and the medical doctors had been unable to prescribe a cure. Fear and pain had etched deep lines into her pretty face.

"I can't sleep," she said. "I can't even close my eyes for a minute without seeing horrible animals rushing at me."

Her husband explained that whenever his wife fell asleep from sheer exhaustion, she would begin to scream almost immediately.

"I try to shake her awake, but sometimes it takes as long as ten minutes to bring her back to consciousness, and all that time she screams with an anguish that is driving me to despair as well," he said.

I listened to their tragic story and said, "I have only one suggestion. Please kneel with me, and let us thank God that you are just like you are."

They both stared at me as if they were sure I hadn't meant what I said. Carefully I explained how I had learned that God wants us to be thankful for all things.

"Everything that has happened in your life so far has served to bring you to this very point," I said. "I believe God loves you and is going to do something very wonderful for you. Now He wants you to thank Him for everything that has brought you to Him."

I leafed through my Bible and showed them the scriptures I had underlined.

They both accepted what they heard and knelt to thank God for everything in their lives, particularly for the flashbacks from drugs. I could feel the presence of God in the room.

"The Holy Spirit is making it clear that He is healing you right now," I said. I placed my hand on the girl's head and prayed, "Thank you, Lord, for healing this girl right now."

She opened her eyes and looked amazed.

"Something has happened to me. When I closed my eyes to pray I didn't see anything!"

"Jesus has healed you," I said. "Now He wants to come into your life as your Savior. Will you accept him?"

Both the girl and her husband eagerly said, "Yes!" Still on their knees, they asked Jesus to come into their lives. Then they walked out of my office rejoicing.

The girl's healing was permanent. Never again did the flashbacks return. The power of the drug over her mind had been broken by the power of God.

Medical authorities admit their helplessness in dealing with addicts who've spent years in slavery to drugs. Yet in recent years we've been hearing with increasing frequency of drug addicts who've been set free after ten, twenty, or thirty years of heavy dependency on hard drugs. They've been freed by the supernatural intervention of God in their lives.

This kind of change cannot be brought about by a new attitude or a determined effort of self-will. This is God's power at work in human lives.

Any form of sincere prayers opens the door for God's power to move into our lives. But the prayer of praise releases more of God's power than any other form of petition. The Bible gives examples which demonstrate this fact again and again.

"But thou art holy, O thou that inhabitest the praises of Israel," we read in Psa. 22:3 (KJV). No wonder God's power and presence is near when we praise Him. He actually dwells, inhabits, resides, in our praises!

A remarkable example of how God works while we praise Him is found in II Chron. 20.

Jehoshaphat was king of Judah, and one day he discovered that his little kingdom was surrounded by the powerful armies of his enemies—the Moabites, the Ammonites and the Meunites. Jehoshaphat knew that little Judah didn't have a chance in its own might, and he cried out to God:

"We have no might to stand against this great company that is coming against us. We do not know what to do, but our eyes are upon You" (II Chron. 20:12 *Amplified Bible*).

An important step in the act of praising God is to take our eyes off the threatening circumstances and look to God instead. Notice that Jehoshaphat wasn't just closing his eyes to the threat against his kingdom or pretending the enemies weren't there. He took careful stock of the situation, recognized his own helplessness, and turned to God for help.

We are not to be blind to the very real threats of evil in our lives. Seeing them for what they are only gives us greater cause to praise and thank God for working in them with perfect control and authority. But we are not to be preoccupied with the appearance of evil around us. See it, admit our helplessness to cope with it in our own strength, then turn to God.

God said to Jehoshaphat, "Be not afraid or dismayed at this great multitude; for the battle is not yours, but God's" (II Chron. 20:15 *Amplified Bible*).

Now that is a tremendous statement, I think. We don't have the power to deal with the circumstances of our lives, so obviously, the battle isn't ours, but God's!

"You shall not need to fight in this battle; take your position, stand still, and see the deliverance of the Lord . . . "

What a promise! Now what kind of position did God want Jehoshaphat to hold while he was to stand still and watch God at work?

The next morning Jehoshaphat gave the orders to his army. "He appointed singers to sing to the Lord and praise Him in their holy [priestly] garments, as they went out before the army, saying, Give thanks to the Lord, for His mercy and lovingkindness endure for ever!" (II Chron. 20:21 *Amplified Bible*).

This scene took place right in front of the massed ranks of the enemy-armies ready to slaughter the men of Judah. Can you imagine the reaction of their captains as they saw the small band of singers coming out on the battlefield against them?

I've been a chaplain in the army for many years, and I've seen men prepare for many battles. But I've never seen a commanding general order his troops to stand still right in front of the enemy lines while a special band of singers went out ahead singing praises to God.

It sounds like a pretty farfetched idea, doesn't it? It is in this kind of situation that our understanding is most likely to balk.

"It's all well and good to praise the Lord when we're in a tough spot," we may say, "but let's not be ridiculous. God helps those who help themselves. The least we can do is to go out there and fight as valiantly as we know how. Then we'll leave the rest to Him."

But what happened to Jehoshaphat and his men?

"And when they began to sing and to praise, the Lord set ambushments against the men . . . who had come against Judah, and they were [self-] slaughtered" (II Chron. 20:22-23 *Amplified Bible*).

I think it is permissible to assume that if Jehoshaphat had decided that "he better play it safe" and had ordered his men to fight, the outcome would have been very different.

Many of us are constantly defeated by the circumstances around us because we aren't ready to accept that the battle is God's, not ours. Even when we realize our own powerlessness to cope with the enemy, we are afraid to let go and trust ourselves to God's power. This is where

11

we've allowed our own understanding to assume the wrong position in our lives. We say, "I don't understand; therefore I don't dare believe."

God's Word makes it clear that the only way out of *that* dilemma is the step of faith on our part. Believing that God's promises are valid, accepting them, and daring to trust in them leads to understanding. The principle in the Bible is very clear here: Acceptance comes *before* understanding.

The reason for this is simple. Our human understanding is so limited that we can't possibly grasp the magnitude of God's plan and purpose for His creation. If our understanding had to come before our acceptance, we'd never be able to accept very much.

Jehoshaphat would never have dared follow God's plan for the battle if he had insisted on understanding it. God's proposal and promise undoubtedly staggered and went beyond Jehoshaphat's understanding. But Jehoshaphat, we read in the account, was a man who *believed* and trusted God. With his understanding, he relied on and trusted God.

Joshua was another leader who received battle orders from God that must have staggered his understanding and challenged his willingness to accept what must have seemed absurd to many who watched.

We've all sung, "Joshua fought the battle of Jericho—and the walls came tumbling down."

The city of Jericho was a fortified stronghold, and the Israelites who had wandered for forty years in the wilderness certainly didn't have the weapons or the power to take the city. But Joshua believed God when He promised to deliver the enemies of Israel into their hands.

God told Joshua to march around Jericho six days in a row. On the seventh day they were to blow their trumpets and shout. "And the wall of the enclosure shall fall down in its place, and the people shall go up [over it] every man straight before him" (Josh. 6:5 *Amplified Bible*).

Joshua trusted God, but I wonder what you or I would have thought and said if we'd been among his followers. Would we have grumbled and balked at his foolhardy suggestion? I wonder what the inhabitants of Jericho thought as they stood on the sturdy fortified walls of their city and watched the Israelites march around, carrying the Ark of the Covenant with them.

At one time I used to think that the story of Joshua and the battle of Jericho was a mixture of myth, exaggeration, and fairy tale. But archeologists have located the ruins of old Jericho in recent years, and found ample evidence that the walls of the city did collapse at a time in history corresponding to the biblical record. The walls of Jericho *did* come tumbling down. The power of God was at work while His people showed their trust and confidence by praising Him with trumpets and shouts.

The examples of Jehoshaphat and Joshua clearly demonstrate that God wins our victories by means and principles that look utterly foolish and contradictory to our human wisdom and strategies.

We are told to trust Him, praise Him, and watch Him work. This is essentially how Jesus Christ operated during His time of ministry in Israel. He openly admitted that of Himself He could do nothing; His part was to submit to His Father's will in perfect obedience, trust, and faith, so that God's power could meet the needs of the people.

We may take a look at a couple of Jesus' prayers concerning a difficult problem.

There was the case of the 5,000 who had followed Him out of town to hear Him preach. They were hungry. The only food available was one little boy's lunch—five loaves of bread and two fishes.

How did Jesus pray? Did He plead with God to perform a miracle?

"He looked up to heaven, and praising God gave thanks, and broke the loaves, and kept on giving them to the disciples to set before the people; and He [also] divided the two fish among [them] all. And they all ate and were satisfied. And they took up twelve . . . baskets full of broken pieces [from the loaves] and of the fish" (Mark 6:41-43 *Amplified Bible*).

Some of us may object here and say, "But that was Jesus; He *knew* what God could do. It wouldn't work for us!"

But Jesus told his followers, "In solemn truth I tell you, anyone believing in me shall do the same miracles I have done, and even greater ones, because I am going to be with the Father. You can ask him for anything, using my name, and I will do it, for this will bring praise to the Father . . . " (John 14:12-13).

Jesus said we could do *greater* things. Does that mean that God possibly has a plan concerning famines around the world and the projected food shortage that environmentalists and agricultural experts so solemnly predict?

Yes, I do believe it does. I know of several instances where people have taken God at His Word, thanked Him, and praised Him for a limited food supply, and seen it stretch to feed many more than it was originally projected for.

When Jesus was confronted with the death of Lazarus, he again prayed a simple prayer of thanksgiving. When the stone was rolled away from the grave opening where Lazarus had been buried for four days, Jesus lifted His eyes and said, "Father, thank you for hearing me" (John 11:41). Then He commanded Lazarus to come from the grave. And the man who had been dead four days walked out!

The Bible says that Jesus came to earth to make it possible for us to praise God. Isaiah the prophet foretold Jesus' coming and said that He would come "to preach the Gospel of good tidings . . . to bind up and heal the brokenhearted, to proclaim liberty to the [physical and spiritual] captives, and the opening of the prison and of the eyes to those who are bound . . . to grant [consolation and joy] to those who mourn . . . the oil of joy for mourning, the garment . . . of praise instead of a heavy, burdened and failing spirit" (Isa. 61:1-3 *Amplified Bible*).

You may recognize your own condition on the list. Are you brokenhearted? Bound by physical limitations, sickness, spiritual limitations? In physical prison, or imprisoned by your own spiritual blindness? Are you mourning? Unable to rejoice, be thankful, or praise God? Is your spirit heavily burdened and failing?

Perhaps it is because you haven't fully accepted and understood the Good News Jesus came to bring.

Praise is an active response to what we *know* that God has done and is doing for us in our lives and in this world through His Son Jesus Christ and the person of the Holy Spirit.

If we doubt in our hearts what God has done and is doing, we cannot wholeheartedly praise Him. Uncertainty about the Good News will always be a barrier to praise. If we want to be able to praise God in everything, we need to be sure our foundation is solid and without cracks of doubt and uncertainty.

2

Hear the Good News!

If I offer you ten cents as a free gift, you probably won't get very excited about it. You may wonder why I'm doing it, and you may even laugh at me. If I give you another dime and tell you again that it is free, you may shake your head, wondering some more, and if I continue giving you dimes until I've given you twenty, your interest may be stimulated, but you will still be at a loss to figure out what I am trying to prove.

If, instead of a dime, I offer you a thousand-dollar bill, I'm sure you will get excited right away; and if I increase the gift to twenty thousand, you will stare at me in amazement as you begin to realize just how fortunate you are. You may cry for joy, and you will probably want to tell someone right away about the wonderful gift you've received. What great news to share with others! As long as you live, you'll want to talk about it.

"Say, did I ever tell you about the twenty thousand dollars I was given, for free!"

God has given us many wonderful gifts. They're free for the asking. But you may only know of them as ten-cent gifts. We don't get excited over ten cents. You heart doesn't beat faster when you think of receiving a dime. You don't cry tears of gratitude and joy when you think of God's goodness. What's wrong? Is it God's gifts? No, you are living in a ten-cent world!

Many church-going people think of God's gift of eternal life as a ten-cent gift. They believe they have to struggle to live a good life to keep their "free gift." Trying hard to live a good life puts them under such a continual strain that they often wonder if trying hard to be a Christian is really worth it.

No wonder they aren't very enthusiastic about sharing the Good News with anyone else. To them it just means going to church on Sunday, staying away from things that might be a lot of fun, and giving their hard-earned cash in the offering plate.

If this is your "salvation," I understand why you spend all your free evenings watching TV. And why you never think of speaking to your neighbor or to a stranger on the street about God's wonderful love for us. As far as you know, God's gift to you is only equivalent to a dime, so why should you be interested in receiving any more? Dime gifts, you can do without.

But if you received a thousand-dollar gift, you'd be hungry for more! And you would tell everyone where they could get theirs.

We all want thousand-dollar gifts. Americans spend billions of dollars every year hoping to win something for nothing. We have a built-in hunger to acquire for ourselves anything of real value.

Now I tell you that God's free gifts to us are worth more than millions of dollars. He doesn't give them only to those who meet some minimum standards of behavior; Christ has already paid the price for every gift God wants to give to us.

"God says, 'I will destroy all human plans of salvation no matter how wise they seem to be, and ignore the best ideas of men, even the most brilliant of them' " (I Cor. 1:19).

Receiving forgiveness of sin and eternal life as a free gift doesn't fit into the normal pattern of life as we know it. We've been conditioned to believe that we only get what we deserve or are willing to pay for. God's plan of giving us a totally free gift seems so impossible to us that we try to attach something to His offer.

"I'll receive His free gift if I do this or that or something else," we say.

"It is from God alone that you have your life through Christ Jesus," wrote Paul. "He was the one who made us acceptable to God; he made us pure and holy and gave himself to purchase our salvation" (I Cor. 1:30).

The major question for you to decide when you hear wonderful news like that is whether or not Christ had the authority and the power to give you eternal life without requiring that you do one thing to deserve it. If you think that He didn't have the power and the authority, then you must do something to get yourself right with God. You will have to strive all your life to be sure you meet His standards. But God's Word declares that no matter how hard you try, you cannot be as good as He demands. Your very effort to prove your own goodness is the same as saying that God is a liar!

"Through Christ, all the kindness of God has been poured out upon us undeserving sinners; and now he is sending us out around the world to tell all people everywhere the great things God has done for them" (Rom. 1:5), wrote Paul.

Paul had received some of the "thousand-dollar bills," and he was excited! He was determined to let the whole world know.

"This Good News tells us that God *makes us ready* for heaven—makes us right in God's sight—when we put our faith and trust in Christ to save us" (Rom. 1:17).

Paul said that *God makes us ready.* When God does it, can you depend on it being done right? Will there be any room for improvement? Are you ready to face Him at the end of this life if you are what *He has made you?*

We can't make ourselves good enough, no matter how hard we try.

"No one can *ever* find God's favor by being good enough. For the more we know of God's laws, the clearer it becomes that we don't obey them" (Rom. 3:20).

The more you learn about what is right, the more you will be aware of how unrighteous you are. Only the proud of heart feel that they have made it to some state of personal goodness. Christ is the only unselfish, sinless force in the world. Only *His presence in you* makes you any better than the most sinful person who ever lived!

"Then what can we boast about doing, to earn our salvation? Nothing at all. Why? Because our acquittal is not based on our good deeds; it is based on *what Christ has done and our faith in him.* So it is that we are saved by faith in Christ and not by the good things we do" (Rom. 3:27-28).

Paul emphasized that this doctrine of faith was nothing new. He pointed out that Abraham was never accepted by God because of his good deeds, but because of his faith.

Abraham was not a *good* man, even by the moral standards of his day. When he was going into an alien country, he knew that the people there might decide to rob him of some of his possessions, his cattle, or even his beautiful wife. So to make his journey safer, he decided to introduce his wife, Sarah, as his sister. This way, he reasoned, any dangerous male suitors would show him favors instead of trying to kill him. Sure enough, it happened as Abraham had expected. The king himself saw Sarah and wanted her for his wife. She was brought to his palace, and Abraham was bestowed with fine gifts.

Now what did Abraham do? Make plans to rescue his wife? Not at all. He simply enjoyed his good fortune. God Himself had to intervene and show the king that Abraham had been deceitful.

Would you accept Abraham as a member of your church? Consider the question carefully.

God accepted Abraham, not because he lived up to the moral standards, obviously, but because Abraham believed God. His faith was accepted as all the goodness he needed. Abraham may not be good in your eyes, but he was good in God's eyes, because he believed.

You may think more of your own goodness than you do of Abraham or of some people you know, but in God's eyes, man's sinfulness is total and complete. Degrees of goodness and badness cannot determine our salvation or our usefulness in God's kingdom. Abraham didn't earn his way to heaven by being good.

Paul wrote, "For being saved is a gift; if a person could earn it by being good, then it wouldn't be free—but it is! It is given to those who do not work for it. For God declares sinners to be good in his sight if they have faith in Christ to save them from God's wrath" (Rom. 4:5).

We are made *good in God's sight!*

If you really believed this, would you be excited about it? Would you want to tell others how simple it is to become a Christian? Just think of it: around you are millions of people who actually believe that to become a Christian they must be good enough. And they know only too well that they can never manage to become good enough. How desperate and bleak their future must look. How they need to hear the Good News.

God's gift is free! Paul wrote, "If it is by God's kindness [we are saved], then it is not by their being good enough. For in that case the free gift would no longer be free—it isn't free when it is earned" (Rom. 11:6).

The Good News should be proclaimed everywhere, and yet most Christians are curiously tongue-tied when it comes to talking about it.

Have you ever gone up to a stranger and asked for directions to a bus station or to Joe's Pizza Parlor? Were you scared when you did it? Did your heart pound and your tongue feel dry and swollen? Of course not. Then why do you feel that way when you think of telling a stranger what Jesus Christ has done for him?

God wants us to share the Good News with everyone. Jesus told His disciples to go out and tell the whole world what He has done for us. So who do you think wants to keep it a secret?

Yes, there is an enemy prowling around, and his favorite trick is to make us fearful of sharing the wonderful news about God's free gifts. But if we are absolutely certain of what God has done for us, if we've accepted some of His free "thousand-dollar bills," then we are going to bubble over with the news.

Some people will still worry about how good God requires us to be once we've been forgiven of our sins and have received the free gift of eternal life. Paul wrote about that to the Romans.

"Now then, the question: Is this blessing given only to those who have faith in Christ but also keep the Jewish laws, or is the blessing also given to those who do not keep the Jewish rules, but only trust in Christ? Well, what about Abraham? We say that he received these blessings through his faith. Was it by faith alone? Or because he also kept the Jewish rules?" (Rom. 4:9).

Paul draws an amazing conclusion: Abraham did not keep the law, because there was no law yet given!

It is clear then, that God's promise to give the whole earth to Abraham and his descendants was not because Abraham obeyed God's laws but because he trusted God to keep his promise (Rom. 4:13).

God has promised us an inheritance, too, not if we're good, but if we believe Him. You may not think that God's plan is a very good solution, but it is God's solution to our problem.

The Jews kept excusing themselves and insisted that they were not sinners. Many Christians misunderstand Jesus' answer to the Jews. He insisted that the law of God was far purer than they conceived it to be. They thought they were innocent, for example, of committing adultery. But Jesus explained that if they even looked at a woman and desired her, they had already committed adultery with her. Jesus told them they could tear their eyes out to keep their mind pure. But Jesus knew the mind of man. Even if a man doesn't want to sin, there is another part of him that wants to, and so we are always faced with this inward battle.

So what was Jesus trying to tell us? That we would have to work even harder to try to keep the law? No, He only wanted to show us how much we need Him. Nearly every parable and teaching of Jesus was meant to convince us of our need for a Savior. Paul declared that faith in Christ was the only way to keep the whole law.

If you try to whip your physical being into shape and actually succeed in keeping some of His laws, what have you accomplished? Nothing. Jesus made it clear that unless you keep every law perfectly, you are guilty of breaking them all.

Christ wasn't trying to discourage you, but to encourage you! He said He would do something to deliver you from the problem.

"Christ gives to those who trust in him everything they are trying to get by keeping his laws!" (Rom. 10:4).

When Christ enters your life, you'll still keep your physical body, and with it some of your unholy appetites. But there's a big difference: "When someone becomes a Christian he becomes a brand new person inside. He is not the same any more" (II Cor. 5:17).

You may look much the same, but you *aren't* the same.

19

"Your body will die, because of sin; but your spirit will live, for Christ has pardoned it" (Rom. 8:10).

You've become a new spiritual being inside, because Christ dwells there through the Holy Spirit. Your old physical body will one day die, but you won't. You will live forever, with Christ.

I have talked to thousands of church-going people and asked them what they thought a man must do in order to get to heaven. I've asked the question in some of the most fundamental, Bible-believing churches in our country and heard the same answer over and over.

Ninety-nine out of every hundred have told me about the things we must *do*. Keep the commandments, go to church, give your money, don't mistreat others, etc.—a never-ending list of what *they* are trying to do.

Church-going people have heard and believed the lie that salvation depends on what *we* do. No wonder the spreading of the Good News has gone slow. Who wants to come to church, receive ten cents, and then go out to tell the world about it?

Are you still convinced that God has offered you only ten-cent gifts? Have you thought that to receive God's blessings you have to have faith—plus something?

"So if you still claim that God's blessings go to those who are 'good enough,' then you are saying that God's promises to those who have faith are meaningless, and faith is foolish" (Rom. 4:14).

Paul wrote, "But the fact of the matter is this: when we try to gain God's blessing and salvation by keeping his laws we *always* end up under his anger, for we *always* fail to keep them" (Rom. 4:15).

Does that mean God gets angry with us for trying to be good and keep His law? Of course not. He gets angry because He knows *why* we're trying to keep His law. If we try to keep the law for fear that God will punish us if we don't, our efforts are worthless. If we try to keep it to deserve any of His blessings, we are striving in vain. So why should we even try to do anything good? Couldn't we just be as bad as we want, since salvation is free anyway?

Now that is of course utterly ridiculous. We should do good, but only because we love God and *want* to please Him. If we fully understand what His wonderful gifts to us are, we will respond to His love by loving Him. If you cling to the idea of trying to do good to deserve God's favor, you may *never* learn to love Him. You surely will never get excited about the "thousand-dollar bills."

"Now God has shown us a different way to heaven—not by 'being good enough' and trying to keep his laws, but by a new way (though not new, really, for the scriptures told about it long ago). Now God says He will accept and acquit us—declare us 'not guilty'—if we trust

Jesus Christ to take away our sins. And we can all be saved in this same way, by coming to Christ, no matter who we are or what we have been like" (Rom. 3:21-22).

The condition is, "*if we trust Jesus Christ.*" To trust in yourself to be either "good enough" or not "too bad," is exactly the opposite.

What did Jesus Christ do for us?

"God sent Christ Jesus to take the punishment for our sins and to end all God's anger against us. He used Christ's *blood* and our *faith* as the means of saving us from his wrath" (Rom. 3:25).

Both of these elements are essential. One without the other won't do the job. Christ did the doing, but that won't help us if we don't respond by believing. If we get tangled up in the "doing," we will never be free to do the believing.

"He died for our sins and rose again to make us right with God, filling us with God's goodness" (Rom. 4:25). "Sin ruled over all men and brought them to death, but now God's kindness rules instead, giving us right standing with God and resulting in eternal life through Jesus Christ our Lord" (Rom. 5:21).

Our choice is clearly between God's kindness or His just judgment. We are offered the free gift of eternal life, and the alternative is plainly death.

I remember an attractive young army nurse stationed at a hospital in Vietnam where I was chaplain. The nurse arrived full of life and vitality, but soon her happy smile faded away. She could not bear to see the young soldiers come back from the battlefront badly wounded and in pain. She often came to my office to speak about her feelings.

"How can you say that God loves these men when He lets them suffer so?" she asked me one day.

"It would be easier if you gave your worries and concern for your patients to God and trusted Him to help them," I suggested. "God loves these wounded soldiers far more than you and I are capable of."

The nurse shook her head.

"I can't, Chaplain," she said. "Maybe someday, but not now. It hurts too much to look at the suffering. I can't thank God for it now."

Her visits to the chaplain's office became less frequent. From the dull expression in her once bright eyes, I began to suspect that she was taking pills to fight her depression. She no longer seemed to respond to what was going on around her. She was transferred, and I lost track of her.

Just recently I received a letter from a state reformatory for women in a midwestern state.

"Dear Chaplain:

"I've traveled many miles in the wrong direction since I last saw you at the hospital in Vietnam. I seem to have lost the decent part of myself on the way. After Vietnam I couldn't find peace of mind, and I started to drift.

"It all began while I was watching the useless deaths and maiming of young bodies in the hospital. I blamed God for it all, and now I realize that by blaming Him I cut myself off from Him and destroyed myself. Now I am not able to respond to anything or anyone. I'm just existing in a grey, feelingless void.

"I know that God is the answer. I've fought it for many years, but now I know. I've wanted to write you for some time, but I've been ashamed. I remember how good it felt to be able to talk in the chaplain's office. I didn't want to accept the answer then. I hope it isn't too late. Please pray for me . . . "

The young nurse had turned away from the gift God held out for her. Now she had come to recognize the consequences. But think of all the suffering she must have endured.

Receiving Christ's gift of eternal life is one of the easiest things you will ever do! There is nothing difficult about it. You don't have to be clever or good—even a little child can do it!

Paul wrote, "Salvation that comes from trusting Christ . . . is already within easy reach of each of us; in fact, it is as near as our own hearts and mouths. For if you tell others with your own mouth that Jesus Christ is your Lord, and believe in your own heart that God has raised Him from the dead, you will be saved" (Rom. 10:8-9).

So why do some people hesitate? What are they afraid of?

The young army nurse was afraid to trust herself to a God who could let young soldiers be killed and maimed in battle. She didn't trust God's love.

"We need have no fear of someone who loves us perfectly," wrote John. "His perfect love for us eliminates all dread of what he might do to us. If we are afraid, it is for fear of what he might do to us, and shows that we are not fully convinced that he really loves us." (I John 4:18).

God *is* love. Everything He does is love in action. Our problem is we have such a limited picture of what love is all about. We've all been hurt and disappointed by human love, the kind that rewards us and accepts us when we're good and punishes and rejects us when we're bad. But that is not like God's love at all.

The Greek version of the New Testament uses two words that we translate simply as "love." One is *philia,* brotherly love; it means a deep, instinctive, personal affection. The other is *agape*, divine love. It is the kind Paul says that husbands and wives should have for each other, and *agape* is used to describe God's love for us. It means a reasoning, intentional, deliberate, spiritual devotion. It doesn't originate in feelings or emotions; it is a deliberate act of love, originating in the will. It never changes and can always be relied on, because it doesn't depend on how lovable or deserving the loved one is.

That is how God loves us. He loves us when we reject Him, when we disobey, and when we're mean. He loves us when we've made a mess of our lives, and He is always ready to accept and forgive us and to fill us with His joy and peace.

The free gift of God's love is eternal life in Christ Jesus, and it is as near to us as our mouth and our heart. We simply accept what Jesus has done for us, believe in our heart that He lives, and tell others about it. It is so simple, yet some stop short even when they *know* what the gift is all about.

Nicodemus, a religious and devout Jew, came to Jesus one night and asked Him how he could enter the kingdom of God. Nicodemus knew that Jesus was sent of God and had the answer.

Jesus told him, " 'With all the earnestness I possess I tell you this: Unless you are born again, you can never get into the Kingdom of God'

" 'Born again!' exclained Nicodemus. 'What do you mean? How can an old man go back into his mother's womb and be born again?'

"Jesus replied, 'What I am telling you so earnestly is this: Unless one is born of water and the Spirit, he cannot enter the Kingdom of God. Men can only reproduce human life, but the Holy Spirit gives new life from heaven.' "

Nicodemus *knew* who Jesus was, but that wasn't enough. It is necessary also to act on what we know and to accept Jesus Christ as our personal Savior by inviting Him into our lives. When He comes in, by the Holy Spirit, we are spiritually born again. We can only communicate with God in our spirit, and so we must be born again in order to be equipped to know God. If we're not born again, we're still spiritually dead.

Paul wrote, "I have been crucified with Christ: and I myself no longer live, but Christ lives in me. And the real life I now have within this body is a result of my trusting in the Son of God, who loved me and gave himself for me" (Gal. 2:20).

Paul told the Corinthians, "Check up on yourselves. Are you really Christians? Do you pass the test? Do you feel Christ's presence and power more and more within you? Or are you just pretending to be Christians when actually you aren't at all?" (II Cor. 13:5).

Are you really a Christian? Have you been born again?

There are many like Nicodemus in our churches today. They spend time studying the scriptures and praying daily; they attend Bible studies and prayer groups and teach Sunday School. Some are even preachers.

They may have grown up in church, and call themselves "born" Methodist, Presbyterian, Lutheran, Catholic, Pentecostal, Baptist, or whatever denomination they happen to be in.

They know all *about* Christianity. They know that Jesus is the Son of God who died for their sins; they know He lives again; but they've never actually surrendered *their* lives to Him and invited Him to be Lord and Savior in *their* hearts. Thousands of people regularly attend worship services and go through all the outward forms of Christianity without ever having experienced Christ *in* their lives.

The gift of salvation and eternal life is absolutely free; you can do nothing to earn it or deserve it, but you *must* receive it before it can become yours. In love God reaches out, lovingly arranges circumstances to show us how much we need Him, and draws us to Himself.

Once a Christian sergeant brought a soldier from his platoon to my office. The soldier was facing a dishonorable discharge and a prison term for using and dealing in drugs. He'd been an addict since his early teens, and the time he spent in the army had only made matters worse. He had served in Vietnam where dope was as easy to come by as chewing gum.

"I've made a mess of my life, and it's too late to change," he said. The look in his eyes was dark and desperate.

"What about God?" I asked. "He's got the power to change you."

The soldier shrugged.

"Why should He," he said. "I've never done anything for Him."

"He loves you," I said. "He sent Jesus to take the punishment for everything you've ever done. He can heal you, too."

The soldier looked glum.

"I've heard about Jesus," he said. "I'd like to ask Him to be my Savior, but I don't think it will do any good now. I can't stop using dope no matter now hard I try. I've been a junkie too long."

"God can heal you," I said confidently. "Don't you think He is more powerful than dope?"

The soldier looked doubtful.

"Are you willing to try Him?" I asked. The soldier nodded.

"I'll try anything," he said. "I want to get out of the hell I'm in now."

"Then thank God right now for what He's going to do for you in the next few minutes, and thank Him for everything that has happened in your life to bring you to this spot!"

"Now wait a minute!" The soldier looked upset. "You mean I'm supposed to thank God for everything in my life up to now, even that I'm an addict?"

"It's your addiction that brings you to Him, isn't it?" I said. "If God heals you, forgives you, and gives you a brand-new, eternal life with Jesus, don't you think you can thank Him for everything that made you see you needed Him?"

The dark look of doubt was still in the soldier's eyes.

"Will you let me pray for you?" I asked, and he nodded.

I placed my hands on his head. "Dear Heavenly Father," I prayed. "Thank you for loving this boy and drawing Him to you. Now send your Holy Spirit to help him believe that you've been working in every dark and lonely moment of his life to bring him to Christ."

When I finished there was a new light in the soldier's eyes.

"It is very strange," he said, "but for some reason I really do believe that God has taken everything bad that ever happened to me and is working it for my good."

His eyes were moist, and he bowed his head again, this time praying for himself, asking God to forgive him for his rebellion, and asking Jesus to come and take over his life.

What happened next, defies my ability to explain. I placed my hands on his head again, praying that God would heal him, cleanse his mind of all desire for dope, and fill him instead with His love. I felt a force flow through to the young soldier. His face brightened like a child's, and tears flowed down his cheeks.

"It has happened!" he shouted. "I don't need dope anymore—Jesus lives in me!"

For the young soldier it was the moment of rebirth. He would never be the same again. He was born again, not because he *felt* the presence of Jesus, but because he made a decision to trust God.

If our relationship with God was dependent on our feelings, it really wouldn't be our choice, would it? We can't choose how we're going to feel. But we *can* choose to trust, to believe, and to have faith. We are saved by *faith*, the Bible says. But many of us have a very distorted picture of faith.

"I just don't have faith to believe," we say, and what we really mean is, "I don't *feel* sure."

Faith and feelings are *not* the same.

"Now faith is the assurance (the confirmation, the title-deed) of the things [we] hope for, being the proof of things [we] do not see and the conviction of their reality—faith perceiving as real fact what is not revealed to the senses" (Heb. 11:1 *Amplified Bible).*

Faith does not originate in our emotions, our feelings, or our senses. Faith is a matter of *will.* We decide to perceive as real fact what is *not* revealed to our senses.

To be saved by *faith,* means that we accept Jesus Christ as our Savior by an act of our will, not by our emotions or feelings. We are born again by faith, saved by faith, and that means we take God's promise that it has happened once we've accepted Christ into our hearts. We may not *feel* saved or *feel* born again, but that doesn't change the fact that we *are*.

We've talked about how easy it is to make our understanding a stumbling block to faith. It is just as dangerous to try to measure our faith by feelings. We've been confusing feeling with fact for so long that we think we *are* what we *feel*. I *feel* sick—so I must *be* sick. But our feelings are changeable and can be affected by the weather, by our diet, by our sleep, or the mood of our boss. Our feelings are a poor test of reality. When we apply them as a test of our relationship with God, we get into trouble.

Jesus said, "Pray in faith, *believing* you have received." We can't pray the prayer of faith if we insist on measuring the results by our feelings. We may discover that God's truth in the Bible often says we should do the exact opposite of what we feel.

"Love your enemies," said Jesus.

Didn't He know how we *feel* about our enemies? Sure He does. But He's telling us that we don't have to let our feelings boss us around anymore. We're free to choose to love even our enemies!

We are also free to accept God's Word as fact for us, regardless of what our emotions, our senses, our intellect, or our feelings try to tell us. Our new life in Jesus Christ is a life in *faith*. That means a life in freedom from the tyranny of our own emotions, intellect, and senses. We don't have to pay attention to them anymore!

The Bible tells us we can be saved by faith, healed by faith, justified by faith, shielded by faith, walk in faith, stand in faith, live by faith, inherit the promises of God by faith, be rich in faith, pray in faith, overcome the world by faith, praise God by faith.

Our salvation experience becomes an accomplished fact when we accept it by faith. God isn't looking at our feelings, but at the decision we made. We may be torn by doubt and feeling terrible, but as long as we accept Christ on faith, God considers the transaction done. Whatever you may feel or not feel immediately following your commitment makes no difference. God accepted your surrender of will, and you were born again by His Holy Spirit.

I'm concerned when people come to me and say, "Oh, I just *know* Jesus touched me today, because I *felt* it." The same people will come back later and say, "I'm not sure I'm saved anymore; I don't *feel* the presence of God."

Praise God when you *do* have a wonderful experience of His presence, but don't let your faith depend on how you feel. A Christian who makes emotional experiences the test of his salvation will always be torn by doubts.

One woman wrote me:

"I gave my life to Jesus Christ several years ago, but nothing happened. I didn't feel anything, and as time went on I lost my hope and quit trying to keep my promise to Jesus about living for Him. Since then my life has become unbearable. I'm so depressed I'm afraid I'll destroy my marriage . . . I've read *Prison to Praise* and know that what I feel is a deep hunger for Christ. I've prayed for forgiveness, and I want to commit myself to Him again. I accept Jesus Christ as my personal Savior and I want very much to be a part of His kingdom. I don't feel any different yet . . . please pray for me, because I can't go on feeling this way much longer . . . "

Another letter came from a young man in a federal prison:

"I believe in Jesus Christ with what I hope to be all my heart; I received Him as my Savior two years ago. I really meant it, and I felt wonderful for two days. Then I slipped right back into my old ways. I've had moments since then when I've felt the same joy, but I can't make it last. I want to serve God, but I just can't seem to find Him. I've read *Prison to Praise* and I know I need what you wrote about. How do I find it? Do you think maybe I don't want it badly enough? How can I make myself want it more? I've made such a mess out of my life. There's no meaning, the way I'm going. I've taken many Bible courses, and I still don't seem to be getting anywhere. I so badly want to find Christ. I'll soon be leaving prison, and I want to go out in the world with His love. Please pray that I may find Him and experience the joy He promised in the Bible . . . "

I've received hundreds of letters just like that, and wherever I go I meet people who say they aren't sure they really met Jesus.

The reason for their doubt is always the same: "I don't *feel* anything."

They are prisoners of their feelings and have greater faith in them than in God's Word. Once we surrender to Jesus, He says about us, "I give them eternal life and they shall never perish. *No one* shall snatch them away from me (John 10:28).

How do we fight our feelings and doubts?

Paul wrote, "The only condition [for salvation] is that you fully believe the Truth, standing in it steadfast and firm, strong in the Lord, convinced of the Good News that Jesus died for you, and never shifting from trusting him to save you. This is the wonderful news that came to each of you and is now spreading all over the world" (Col. 1:23).

When doubts and feelings come to attack our faith, God tells us to stand firmly on His Word.

One lady I know has a very practical way of doing it. When a doubt comes along, she finds a verse in the Bible that tells the truth about the matter. She copies the verse on a piece of paper, and when the doubt comes, she quotes the verse to herself.

The thought would come to her when she felt discouraged, *Are you sure God heard your prayer when you accepted Jesus Christ as your Savior?*

In her Bible she found the verse, "And this is the confidence which we have in him, that if we ask anything according to his will he hears us. And if we know that he hears us in whatever we ask, we know that we *have obtained* the requests made of him" (I John 5:14-15 RSV).

She copied it down, and underneath she wrote, "On January 14, 1969, I confessed my sins and asked Jesus Christ to come into my life as Savior and Lord. I know it happened because my request was in agreement with God's plan and will for my life."

She placed the paper by her bedroom mirror, and when the doubt came, she pointed to the paper and said out loud, "There it is. I *know* I am born again. I *know* God has accepted me, because I accepted His Son as my Savior on that day. I never have to wonder about it again."

When she felt guilt over a specific sin she had already confessed to God, the temptation came to doubt that she'd really been forgiven. She checked her Bible and wrote, "If we confess our sins to him, he can be depended on to forgive us and to cleanse us from every wrong. [And it is perfectly proper for God to do this for us because Christ died to wash away our sins]" (I John 1:9).

Underneath she wrote down the sin she had confessed, with the date and the words, "Hallelujah, I'm forgiven!"

Gradually her doubts ceased completely.

You can fight your doubts and feelings by keeping a written, dated record of your prayer-transactions, along with a Bible verse stating God's promise.

If you've been a Christian for several years, but still have recurring doubts about your salvation or your commitment, don't let your doubts and feelings fool you any longer. Make a recommitment right now and put it in writing with today's date. Some people record important spiritual milestones in their Bibles.

The Christian life is a continuous journey in faith. It is a good idea to keep a record of the way we've gone. It serves as a useful reminder on dark days when we feel sure we haven't moved at all. Looking back, we can praise and thank God for the way He's brought us.

Our faith is built on God's fact, not on feeling. But God's promise is also that we will experience more and more of His joy and peace in our lives as we go along. Rejoice when that happens, but rejoice also when you feel dry and empty.

Your salvation is still a wonderful fact. Throw the switch of your willpower in God's direction and say, "I will to believe, God. I stand on your Word."

Do it, and discover that your old dependency on feeling will gradually fade away. You will be free to believe!

"You will know the truth," Jesus promised, "and the truth will set you free" (John 8:32).

Accept God's Word as truth—and you will be free!

3

Power Unlimited

When we give our trust over to Christ, what actually happens?

"God . . . has blessed us with every blessing in heaven because we belong to Christ" (Eph. 1:3).

Because we belong to Christ we are children of God. We have entered His kingdom, and all the power, privileges, and rights belonging to the children of God are ours.

Just look at all the provisions our Father in heaven has made for us—"every blessing in heaven." Not because we are worthy in our own strength, *but because we belong to Christ!*

A human baby doesn't grow by stretching himself. He doesn't have to be good to deserve his daily care. He is fed, clothed, loved, and cared for by his mother and father, simply because he is their child. They know his every need, and they provide for him. His growth comes about naturally, effortlessly, as long as the child accepts his food and gets his proper rest and exercise.

Can you imagine a human child refusing to eat and sleep, telling his mother, "I'm not ready yet, Mom. I'm over here stretching. When I've grown five inches on my own, I'll be ready to eat."

But that is exactly the way many Christians behave. God has made all the provisions; He's prepared everything we need to grow—food, rest, love, care. But we're over in the corner, struggling and stretching, trying to grow so we'll be worthy to receive.

God decided to do this for us long before you and I were born.

"Long ago, even before he made the world, God chose us to be his very own, through what Christ would do *for us;* he decided then to make us holy . . . " (Eph. 1:4).

Wait a minute! Who is God making *holy?* Have you known anybody

He's made holy yet? If not, do you think He is behind on His schedule? Has He started making *you* holy yet?

Read further: " . . . without a single fault . . . "

Do you think it is possible for God to decide to make Christians be without a single fault and fail so miserably with all the people you know?

But read on: " . . . *in His eyes!*" God has made us holy and without a single fault " . . . in His eyes." He has done a great thing for us. He has changed us "in His eyes." *He* sees us differently. He alone has the power to see the new man. Who can see through the eyes of God? No one but God Himself. He has made a new creature for His own glory and praise.

When others look at you, they may see the same old you. They are not God. You may look at yourself in the mirror and be convinced that you are not holy or without a single fault, but remember that *you* are not God.

Do you dare say that God cannot see what He wants to see? Do you care more about seeing yourself as holy, or in having God see you as holy? Thousands, perhaps millions, of Christians are trying to force themselves into a holy mold to be seen by others or themselves. When they fail, as they inevitably must, the pangs of discouragement overcome them. I've seen their unhappy faces all over the country and heard their confession of failure so often that I know what is coming before they even begin.

How did God do such a fantastic thing as to make us holy in His eyes? Paul says, "We who stand before him covered with his love" (Eph 1:4). A blanket of love! He drops it over us and then stands back to look. What does He see? His own love!

Others may see you. You may see you. God sees His own love! Isn't that enough to start the joybells ringing in your heart, turning your life into thanksgiving and praise?

Why did God do such a marvelous thing for us? Why indeed? "He did this because He wanted to" (Eph. 1:5), Paul stated matter-of-factly. God *wanted* to wrap us in a blanket of His love. Don't you believe that He has the right and authority to give us *anything* He wants to? Every blessing in heaven? Thousand-dollar gifts?

Why did *He* choose to do it Himself? I am convinced that this was the only way He could be sure that His work would be perfect. If He had to depend on you and me doing it right, He would never have had anything worthwhile to present to His Son. The end product was to be for God's glory and not for man's.

Paul wrote, "God's purpose in this was that we should praise God and give glory to him for doing these mighty things for us" (Eph. 1:12).

The result of placing our complete faith in what Christ does for us is glorious.

"Now we can come fearlessly right into God's presence, assured of his glad welcome when we come with Christ and trust in him" (Eph. 3:12).

Too many prayers are made with a whining, self-effacing, false humility. We don't need to apologize to God for being human. He knows all about what we're like. He has watched billions of human beings and knows all of our weaknesses. Now He wants us to believe that through Christ we have the *right* to approach Him and ask for whatever we need.

God wants to bless us with *good* things; He wants us to be happy; and this is sometimes hard for Christians to understand. I grew up in poverty, and our family often received gifts of charity. I grew up resenting it when people wanted to give me things or do something for me, unless I was absolutely sure they *wanted* to do it. I wanted to earn or deserve everything I got. This carried over into my relationship with God. Somehow I wasn't able to believe that God wanted to give me anything more than my immediate needs. *After all,* I reasoned, *why should He?* My vision of God's boundless love and concern for my well-being was rather limited.

Then one day when I was stationed at Fort Benning as a chaplain, I found myself far away in another state without any means of getting back to my station in time to carry out my duties as I had promised. Bad weather had canceled the flight I had planned to travel on, and the next scheduled flight would not get me home on time. To go by car was out of the question. I was grounded, and quite unhappy about it. As long as I had been a chaplain, I had never accepted any speaking engagements that would keep me from my regular duties at the base, and now it looked as if I would have to neglect my job.

I prayed, "Lord, you know I've never been late before; I place this entire situation into your hands. I know you've got a perfect plan for me. I thank you and know that you will meet my needs."

At the meeting where I was speaking, I met an air-force pilot. He was stationed at a base nearby, and when he heard of my plight, he said, "I'm going to call my commander and see if anything can be done."

The commander responded to his request, "Why sure. I need to get in some flying time myself; I'll be glad to fly the chaplain to Fort Benning. Bring him to the base at 0600 tomorrow morning."

I spent the night as a guest in the pilot's home, and the next morning at 6 a.m. we walked onto the airfield. I felt refreshed, and rejoiced that God had met my needs. Just how abundantly He had met them, I didn't quite realize yet.

I looked all over for the plane I expected to see. A row of huge four-engine planes was lined up, but nothing that looked like it was ready to be taken up on a routine flight just to put in flying time. I expected something small and not too comfortable, just something to get me home on time. That was all I needed, I thought.

My pilot friend stopped and said, "Here it is, Chaplain, step aboard."

I looked up. Before me was the biggest airplane on the runway! It seemed to be a block long.

This can't be for me, Lord! I thought. I walked up the steps in a half-daze and followed the crew member who showed me to a comfortable seat in a large lounge. I was the only passenger, and the plane was outfitted with every possible convenience. This was no cargo or transport plane.

The commander came back to introduce himself and said he hoped I would enjoy the flight. I could only mumble my thanks; I was still overwhelmed. I knew that God had provided the plane to bring me back to Fort Benning on time, but why this huge luxury plane? Why hadn't He just picked a small, adequate plane?"

I felt very undeserving, and a quick thought that such a big plane was really a waste went through my head.

"What does it all mean, Lord?" I asked, bewildered.

"Only that I love you," came the concise answer. "I want to show you that this is how I want to provide for all my children who trust me."

"I am beginning to understand, Lord," I mused, joy welling up in me as the thoughts continued.

"I want you to tell everyone who will listen to be thankful for every detail of their lives, and I will open the windows of heaven and pour out more goodness than they can ever ask for or hope for."

"Thank you, Lord," I chuckled in my seat.

"And remember," the voice continued in my mind, "you can never deserve my blessings. You cannot work for them or earn them. I must give everything to you as a free gift, and because of my own goodness, and you must learn to understand and accept that!"

Whenever I traveled on commercial planes, I landed ten miles from my office, but the huge four-engine plane landed at Fort Benning, within a few hundred yards of where I had an appointment. As I entered the building, I looked at my watch. I had arrived *exactly* on time. Not one minute early or one minute late.

God *does* provide our needs, and He does it abundantly and free. All we have to do is ask. The very *first* free gift God wants His new children to ask for is the baptism in the Holy Spirit.

33

That's right. The baptism in the Holy Spirit was provided as a "first feeding" for newborn believers. They need it to grow.

The Holy Spirit comes to dwell in the new believer the moment He accepts Jesus Christ as his Savior. He is born of the Spirit. But Jesus also told His disciples that they would have to wait until they were *baptized* with the Holy Spirit before they could be His witnesses and spread the Good News with power and authority.

The disciples waited in Jerusalem, just as Jesus had told them, and on the day of Pentecost we read that there came the sound "like a roaring of a mighty windstorm in the skies above them and it filled the house where they were meeting. Then, what looked like flames or tongues of fire appeared and settled on heads. And everyone present was filled with the Holy Spirit and began speaking in languages they didn't know, for the Holy Spirit gave them this ability" (Acts 2:2-4).

This was the beginning of the Christian church. The timid disciples of Christ were now transformed into fearless, bold witnesses; they began immediately to preach the Good News with power and authority, and the same miracles that had followed Christ, followed them.

Jesus said, "Truly, truly I say unto you, he who believes in me will also do the works that I do; and greater works than these will he do, because I go to the Father" (John 14:12 RSV).

New believers were added to the church by the thousands, and when we read the Book of Acts, we see that the baptism in the Holy Spirit usually followed immediately after their conversion. When Peter preached to the household of Cornelius at Caesarea Philippi, the Holy Spirit overwhelmed the listeners as soon as they accepted what Jesus had done for them (Acts 10:44).

When the gospel was preached in Samaria, many Samaritans accepted Jesus as their Savior, and were baptized in water.

Peter and John were sent from Jerusalem, "and as soon as they arrived, they began praying for these new Christians to receive the Holy Spirit" (Acts 8:15).

Peter and John didn't tell the new Christians to wait awhile, or to study scriptures and pray and make themselves ready. The apostles from Jerusalem were concerned that the Spirit had not yet overwhelmed the new believers, and right away, "Peter and John laid their hands upon these believers and they received the Holy Spirit" (Acts 8:17).

The baptism with the Holy Spirit had been promised to everyone who believed in Jesus Christ. Jesus said, " 'If anyone is thirsty, let him come to me and drink. For the Scriptures declare that rivers of living water shall flow from the inmost being of anyone who believes in me.'

(He was speaking of the Holy Spirit, "who would be *given to everyone* believing in him" (John 7:37-39).

The baptism in the Holy Spirit is a free gift. It cannot be earned. Jesus, who provided our salvation, also provided the Holy Spirit.

"I will ask the Father and He will give you another Comforter, and he will never leave you. He is the Holy Spirit," Jesus said (John 14:16-17).

Jesus is the One who sends the Holy Spirit; He baptizes us in the Holy Spirit.

God spoke to John the Baptist when he was baptizing in the river Jordan. "When you see the Holy Spirit descending and resting upon someone—he is the one you are looking for. He is the one who baptizes with the Holy Spirit" (John 1:33).

Then why do so many Christians struggle so desperately to receive the baptism in the Holy Spirit? All over the country I've seen them, sad-faced and unhappy.

"What's wrong with me?" they say, "Am I just too worthless, too weak? I so desperately need the power of God in my life."

A Sunday-school teacher wrote:

"I need the power of the Holy Spirit in my life. I try so hard to become more obedient and Christlike. I thought maybe I wasn't reading enough in my Bible, and I've tried getting up earlier to read for an hour and then pray for half an hour. But I still don't see any power in my life, and I haven't been able to receive the baptism in the Holy Spirit. I've confessed every sin I can think of. I've been a Christian for twenty years, but I am so sadly lacking in Christian virtues that I sometimes wonder if I'm even saved . . . "

Such people are like little babies standing over in a corner trying to stretch and grow so they can eat the wonderful meal that's been prepared for them. They've got miserable hunger pains, but they don't want to eat until they've outgrown their pains.

Christians in the early church had the same problem. They kept thinking they had to make themselves good enough to receive God's free gifts.

Paul wrote:

"Oh, foolish Galatians! What magician has hypnotized you and cast an evil spell upon you? . . . Let me ask you this one question: Did you receive the Holy Spirit by trying to keep the Jewish laws? Of course not, for the Holy Spirit came upon you only after you heard about Christ and trusted Him to save you. Then have you gone completely crazy? For if trying to obey the Jewish laws never gave you spiritual life in the first place, why do you think that trying to obey them now will make you stronger Christians?" (Gal. 3:1-3).

35

The Galatians had already received the Holy Spirit as a result of having trusted Jesus Christ to save them, but the temptation to think of themselves as responsible for their own Christian growth had caused them to turn from a life of faith.

Pride and a temptation to take the credit for our Christian growth lures believers at all stages of our spiritual life. Satan tempts us in two obvious ways. He may whisper, "My, you're getting spiritual! Just try a little harder, and you'll have *more* power." Or he says, "Look how weak and miserable you are! No wonder God can't trust you with more of His blessings!"

You may praise yourself for your spiritual accomplishments, or criticize yourself for your failure—it amounts to the same thing. You are placing the responsibility for your worthiness on yourself instead of on God—where it belongs.

A minister had a weakness he couldn't control, no matter how hard he tried. Finally he ended up in prison convicted of forgery. The minister was a born-again Christian; he was crushed by his own failure, and sincerely repented of his sin. He was able to believe that God had forgiven him, but he was convinced that God could never again use him to bring others to Him.

One day a friend sent him *Prison to Praise.* There he read that God used everything, even our mistakes, for good. With new hope he dared to thank God for his own mistake and imprisonment. He wrote me, "Praise God, my life has changed completely. The old regrets, guilt, and remorse that held me bound are gone. I can praise and thank God for every detail of my life, just as it is. I never before understood the wideness and depth of God's mercy. I once thought of myself as 'good' enough to be used of Him. What a joy it is to die to my old prideful self so that Christ can live in me—and nothing but Christ!"

The minister's cell soon became a temple of praise, and other prisoners were drawn to accept Christ.

When we think of ourselves or others as good enough or not good enough to be used of God, we're falling into a dangerous trap. Jesus warned his followers, "Don't judge and criticize and condemn others, so that you may not be judged and criticized and condemned yourselves."

Only God is qualified to judge, and He has already declared that we are holy and without a single fault in His eyes when we are covered by His love.

How do we dare set up a standard to measure ourselves and others by? Only God is qualified to deal with our sins. However wrong we or others may be, that is a matter for God to deal with.

When we do judge each other, we are often completely wrong. We judge each other by our manner of dress, amount of makeup, our smoking or drinking, what kind of movies we go to.

How do you select a Sunday-school teacher? Imagine two Christians side by side. One is of average height and weight, and you know he smokes. The other weighs at least three hundred pounds; he's a mountain of a man, but he has a kind smile and never forgets to bring his Bible to church.

Now which one of the two would you choose to teach on the subject "How to develop self-discipline as a fruit of the Holy Spirit"?

Smoking is a bad habit, harmful to our health, and it speaks of a lack of self-discipline. And what about the overweight man? The Bible ranks gluttony with drunkenness and says that they both deserve the death penalty! (Deut. 21:20-21). The glutton is hastening his own death, and so is the smoker.

I don't recommend that you should start judging overweight people and smokers. We have no right to judge either.

When the woman caught in adultery was brought to Jesus, the Jewish leaders and Pharisees asked Jesus, "Teacher . . . Moses' law says to kill her. What about it?" Jesus said, "All right, hurl the stones at her until she dies. But only he who never sinned may throw the first!" (John 8:7).

Who among us qualify to pick up stones of criticism, judging, or condemnation? Measuring our "goodness" or "badness" is just another way to try to justify our standing with God by our good works instead of by faith.

When we discuss "faith" and "works," someone usually quotes the verse, "For we are his workmanship, created in Christ Jesus unto good works, which God hath before ordained that we should walk in them" (Eph. 2:10 KJV).

Now doesn't that state plainly that we are born again to do good works for God?

But look at the two verses above that one:

"For by grace are ye saved through faith; and that not of yourselves: it is the gift of God: Not of works, lest any man should boast" (Eph. 2:8-9 KJV).

Does Paul mean that we're saved by faith, but from then on we're on our own? That doesn't make much sense, does it?

Earlier in the letter to the Ephesians Paul said that we've *been made* holy and without a single fault in God's eyes, and that we've been provided with every blessing in heaven.

So what does Paul mean? Maybe he's got a different idea of "works" from what we do.

James wrote, "What is the use (profit), my brethren, for any one to profess to have faith if he has no [good] works [to show for it]? Can [such] faith save [his soul]?...Was not our forefather Abraham [shown to be] justified—made acceptable to God—by [his] works when he brought to the altar as an offering his [own] son Isaac?" (James 2:14, 21 *Amplified Bible*).

Now what kind of good works was that? Walking up on a mountain prepared to sacrifice his only son on the altar because God told him to do it—especially since that was the son through whom God had promised to bless Abraham and give him multitudes of descendants?

James went on to say, "Can't you see that his faith and his actions were, so to speak, partners—that his faith was implemented by his deed? That is what the scripture means when it says: And Abraham believed God, And it was reckoned unto him for righteousness; and he was called the friend of God" (James 2:22-23 Phillips).

So what kind of "good works" are we supposed to do? The disciples once asked Jesus the same question: " 'What are we to do that we may [habitually] be working the works of God?—What are we to do to carry out what God requires?'

"Jesus replied, This is the work (service) that God asks of you, that you *believe in* the One Whom He has sent—that you cleave to, trust, rely on and have faith in His Messenger" (John 6:28-29 *Amplified Bible*).

And that is exactly what Abraham did. Abraham's "good work" was that He trusted God to keep His promises. He never wavered in his faith. And so God chose to make Abraham the father of Israel.

Jesus promised His followers that they would do even greater works than He did, and we know that after receiving the baptism in the Holy Spirit, His followers preached with power and great miracles.

Their part of the great works was to *believe.* The power to perform miracles didn't belong to them, but came from God through them because they believed.

A common misconception about the baptism in the Holy Spirit is that it somehow gives *us* power, that it strengthens *us,* increases *our* power and ability to work for God—that it makes *us* spiritual giants.

Nothing could be further from the truth. So what do we need the baptism for?

The baptism in the Holy Spirit is designed to *reduce* us, so that more of God's presence and power can dwell in us and flow through us.

Paul wrote, "Now glory be to God who by *his mighty power* at work *within us* is able to do far more than we could ever dare to ask or even dream of—infinitely beyond our highest prayers, desires, thoughts, or hopes" (Eph. 3:20).

It is God who does the work in us, and it makes sense that the more we trust in Him and the less we depend on ourselves, the more He is able to do.

So what exactly *is* the baptism in the Holy Spirit?

Jesus often referred to the Holy Spirit as the Spirit of Truth. "When the Holy Spirit, who is truth, comes, he shall guide you into all truth" (John 16:13).

The Holy Spirit of Truth lives in *all* believers and guides them, but to be baptized in the Spirit of Truth means a great deal more. The word we translate as "baptize" in our English Bible actually means to immerse or saturate, and in Greek the same word is used to describe "waterlogged."

So to ask Jesus to baptize us in the Holy Spirit means that we surrender ourselves to be saturated—waterlogged—with His Truth.

Jesus prayed for us to His Father. "Sanctify them—purify, consecrate, separate them for Yourself, make them holy—by the Truth" (John 17:17 *Amplified Bible*).

The baptism in the Holy Spirit is a cleansing, purging, stripping experience; it is total exposure to the searchlight of God's Truth into every little corner of our lives. The baptism is designed to flush out and empty us of our self-reliance, our pride, our little shady areas of deception, and the excuses we've been holding onto—all the things that block our faith and the inflow of God's power and presence in our lives.

The baptism in or with the Holy Spirit serves a twofold purpose: the purging and preparing of the vessel to *contain* God's power and then the *filling* with the power. The two events occur simultaneously, because when the Holy Spirit of Truth begins to saturate our beings, it exposes and drives out all the junk and debris we've let pile up inside us.

Jesus said, "But you shall receive power—ability, efficiency and might—*when* the Holy Spirit has come upon you" (Acts 1:8 *Amplified Bible*).

He didn't mean that the power would belong to us, but it would fill us, and operate through us. We are the containers, the vessels, the channels. However hard we try, we can't become the contents. We are like glasses containing living water. The water can quench men's thirst, but an empty glass can't satisfy anyone.

Paul wrote, "But this precious treasure—this light and power that now shine within us—is held in a perishable container, that is, in our weak bodies. Everyone can see that the glorious power within must be from God and is not our own" (II Cor. 4:7).

To say that we don't need the baptism in the Holy Spirit is the same as to say that we don't need to be cleansed, immersed in, and saturated by God's Truth, nor do we need the fullness of His power operating in and through us.

Jesus told His followers, "You men who are fathers—if your boy asks for bread, do you give him a stone? If he asks for fish, do you give him a snake? If he asks for an egg, do you give him a scorpion? [Of course not!] And if even sinful persons like yourselves give children what they need, don't you realize that your heavenly Father will do at least as much, and give the Holy Spirit to those who ask for him?" (Luke 11:11-13).

So we can ask Jesus to baptize us in the Holy Spirit and *know* that He does it.

Every week I get letters from people who say they've pleaded with God to baptize them in the Holy Spirit, but nothing has happened. What's wrong? The trouble is they are looking at their own feelings instead of at God's fact. The stumbling block is *always* feelings.

The baptism in the Holy Spirit, like every one of God's gifts, must be received in *faith*. That means you may not *feel* anything when it happens. Faith is an act of our will, not a response to feelings.

Now some people experience dramatic physical sensations when they are first baptized in the Holy Spirit, just as some people have a dramatic, emotional encounter with Jesus Christ when they first receive Him as their Savior. But we don't get saved by feeling, and we don't get baptized in the Holy Spirit by feeling either. Whatever outward sensations you may or may not feel when you're baptized in the Holy Spirit, the sensations are *not* the baptism. The baptism is an *inner* transformation.

As a *result* of this inner transformation, we are told in the Bible, there will be plenty of evidence to follow. Increased power and authority in witnessing for Christ, the operation of the gifts of the Holy Spirit through us, the increasing fruit of the Spirit—the love, joy, peace. All these things we'll experience with our senses, but these evidences follow our acceptance of God's fact; we cannot measure them by our feelings.

We must decide to accept God's Word on faith and deliberately turn from paying attention to our feelings. If we don't, we will never be able to exercise our faith.

Tell God that you *will* to take His Word for it. You *will* to believe Jesus baptizes you when you ask Him to. *Stand* firm in your trust and *know* it has happened.

One young man wrote me:

"I am planning to enter seminary next fall, but my Christian life lacks power. I meet with a group of Christians who've experienced the baptism in the Holy Spirit. They pray and speak in tongues, and there are healings and miracles happening. I'm convinced this is all valid according to the scriptures, and I've prayed to receive it, but for some reason or other it hasn't happened to me. I know that the gifts of the Holy Spirit aren't given for our personal enjoyment, but for the work God would have us do. Still, God hasn't trusted me with this experience. What is lacking? I wonder. I believe in the Lord Jesus Christ as my Savior and want to serve Him with all my heart. I've told Him so, many times. I've confessed my sins, both in church and in private prayer, and I know I'm forgiven and cleansed. I want to serve Christ, and I need the baptism in the Holy Spirit to do so effectively. Why then, hasn't it happened? Have I done something wrong so that God doesn't hear my prayer?

"Yesterday I knelt in our prayer meeting and asked that I be allowed to receive the baptism in the Holy Spirit. Several placed their hands on me and prayed that I might receive. But I didn't feel a thing. . . . Please pray for me."

It doesn't matter where you are or what words you use in asking for the baptism in the Holy Spirit. It doesn't matter if you're alone or if someone else prays for you with the laying on of hands. The baptism in the Holy Spirit is a personal matter between you and the Baptizer, Jesus Christ.

You need ask only once, then thank God that He has heard your request and granted it. If you prayed last week and nothing seemed to happen, then you are letting your senses fool you. Jesus did His part; now it is up to you to believe it is done.

You may not feel anything, but there is one tangible consequence you can claim right away and experience the result. The gift of tongues was recorded as a consequence of the baptism in the Holy Spirit in the Book of Acts. It was the *first* operation of a spiritual gift in the newly baptized believers.

When I asked Jesus to baptize me with the Holy Spirit, I didn't feel a thing. A lady laid hands on me and prayed for me in tongues, but I felt no physical sensation then, and thought that nothing had happened. The lady told me to accept the baptism on faith, not to depend on my feelings, and to thank God that it was already done. I did it, but felt a little ridiculous. Then the lady told me I could speak with tongues if I just opened my mouth and let the language pour out. I hesitated and thought that now I was really making a fool of myself. But I knew that the Bible said speaking in tongues *was* a gift of the Holy Spirit, and since I now was filled with the Holy Spirit—whether I could feel it or not—I could expect the Holy Spirit to operate in me and through me. I did notice some strange "words" forming in my mind, and I opened my mouth and said them out loud. They sounded silly, and my instant reaction was to think, *You're faking it Merlin; you're just making up a bunch of gibberish.* Then I realized that speaking *on faith* meant I couldn't rely on my own senses to measure the results. I decided to accept God's word for it and not pay any attention to what *I* thought.

I had still *felt* nothing, but I had made up my mind to *believe.* The first evidence I could register with my feelings was an overwhelming awareness that Jesus Christ was my Savior and Lord. I knew from the Word of God that the Holy Spirit had been sent to witness about Jesus, and I was suddenly convinced more than ever before of Who Jesus was and what He meant to me. The second evidence I felt was a strong sense of love for people. That, too, was foretold in God's Word. Love is a fruit of the Holy Spirit.

Since then I've experienced the operation of some of the other gifts of the Holy Spirit in and through me as well. *I* haven't been given the ability to heal or to perform miracles or to prophesy. I only *believe* that God operates through me in the power of the Holy Spirit when I step out on faith, expecting Him to do so.

When someone is healed after I have laid hands on him and prayed, it is not because I've become extraspiritual. I'm just the channel. When I pray, I sometimes *feel* the presence of God's healing power and sometimes I feel absolutely nothing.

The results never depend on our feelings, only on our faith, that is, our deliberate choice to believe that God is at work.

When you open your mouth and begin to speak in tongues on faith, you will probably be tempted to think just as I did, that you are faking it and making up the words. Don't let that thought fool you into giving up the practice.

If you have sincerely committed yourself and your tongue to God, asking that the Holy Spirit will give you the words to pray, then you can trust that He is doing just that, whether the words sound like made-up nonsense to your ears or not. It isn't really the words that matter anyway, but the fact that the Holy Spirit is praying through us directly to God.

But why then pray at all—in tongues or in English—if God knows what we need before we even ask Him?

We pray, because this is God's plan for His children, and His explicit command to us as well.

"Pray without ceasing" (I Thess. 5:17 KJV).

It is very important that we take time to pray in tongues daily. Just think for a moment what we're actually doing. The Holy Spirit of Truth is speaking through us.

42

Jesus promised that "rivers of living water shall flow from the inmost being of anyone who believes in me" (John 7:38).

He was speaking of the rivers of truth flowing from our innermost being when we have been immersed in and saturated by the Holy Spirit of Truth.

We often think only of the truth that will flow out to others, but think now what the truth first must do in us. Truth is the power that sets our bound-up spirits free. It exposes every hidden lie, every guilt and fear, all the dark areas of our past lurking in the back of our memories, way back in our subconscious soul. We couldn't even begin to talk to God about those things *with our understanding.* And this is one of the reasons *God devised* this new dimension in prayer.

But when we speak in tongues, we communicate directly from our spirit to God. The Holy Spirit prays *for* us, and we bypass the control-center of our own critical understanding. We speak words we don't understand, but the Holy Spirit of Truth searches out the deep areas of our beings. That's what gives speaking in tongues such a great healing power in our own lives. Later we'll discover that when we pray in tongues for others, we pray directly for needs that we don't know anything about with our understanding, and often the people we pray for have no idea what the root of their problem is either.

A housewife who had suffered with serious mental and emotional problems since her early teens accepted Christ as her Savior. But she did not experience a release from the deep tensions that plagued her. She studied what the Bible had to say about the baptism in the Holy Spirit and became convinced God wanted her to experience it.

One day she knelt in her living room and prayed, "I surrender all of me to you, Jesus. Cleanse me of everything that isn't of you, and baptize me in your Holy Spirit. I thank you, and I believe it has been done."

She felt no sensation of any kind and got up from her knees to continue with her housework. But over the next three weeks, something unusual seemed to be going on inside her. She wept almost continuously, and it was as if she was reliving again the early years of her unhappy childhood. Long-forgotten incidents came back to her memory, things others had done to leave scars of hurt and fear, and things she had done to hurt others. With each memory came a surge of repentant tears, and she found herself asking God to forgive her and those who had hurt her and to heal the memories with His love.

She could think of only one explanation for all her tears, the verse in her Bible which read, "And in the same way—by our faith—the Holy Spirit helps us with our daily problems and in our praying. For we don't even know what we should pray for, nor how to pray as we

43

should; but the Holy Spirit prays for us with such feeling and pleads in our behalf with unspeakable yearnings and groanings too deep for utterance" (Rom. 8:26 *Living Bible* and *Amplified Bible*).

In between the crying sessions, she felt increasingly at ease. Then came one evening at the end of the third week when she cried and cried as if her heart was breaking.

"I felt as if the convulsions of tears were coming from the very pit of my being," she recalled. "Then suddenly it eased off, as if a storm had gone away, leaving behing a beautiful calm. I rested in that peace when suddenly I became aware of a light flowing gently over me from above. It could be felt more than seen, and I knew it was the love of God, surrounding me, holding me ... "

Many of her tensions were gone—but not all. Over the next few days she felt lighter at heart than ever before, and she sang to herself as she did her housework or drove errands to town. Over and over she sang a simple chorus she had taught her children. "Oh how I love Jesus, oh, how I love Jesus ... " The song had suddenly taken on a new and happier meaning.

One afternoon she was driving downtown and realized that she was putting make-believe words to the tune she was singing.

"I didn't know what was happening," she said later. "I hadn't really paid much attention to what the Bible had to say about speaking in tongues, but there I was singing in a new language and I suddenly realized it wasn't 'make-believe,' but it had something to do with being baptized in the Holy Spirit."

She continued singing in tongues every day, and as the weeks and months passed, her old tensions and emotional distress vanished.

"The psychiatrist had told me that I would just have to accept myself as an emotional cripple," she said, "but praise God, He healed me. I sang my way to wholeness—in tongues!"

If you have prayed to be baptized in the Holy Spirit, you can take God's Word for it, it is done. You may open your mouth right now and speak whatever words or sounds happen to come to your mind, trusting that it is the Holy Spirit who is placing them in your mind.

God will not force you to speak in tongues. With the baptism in the Holy Spirit, He has given you the ability to speak in tongues, but only if you choose to do so. You use your mouth, your tongue, and your vocal chords, and you can begin speaking and stop speaking at will. If you feel no emotion or sensation of any kind, praise God *for* your lack of feeling. One day you *will* feel, but in the meantime He is giving you a wonderful opportunity to grow in faith.

In your Bible, read everything Jesus had to say about the Holy Spirit; read the Book of Acts and the letters to the young churches concerning the Holy Spirit, the gifts of the Spirit, and the fruit of the Spirit. All that applies to you now.

Expect these things to happen in your own life. Tell God you are willing to be used as a channel for His love to others, and be ready to step out on faith when God provides the opportunities.

Praise God in all circumstances, whether they seem good or bad to you; trust that God is using them to unfold His wonderful plan for your life.

4

Count It All Joy!

"Dear brothers, is your life full of difficulties and temptations? Then be happy, for when the way is rough, your patience has a chance to grow. So let it grow, and don't try to squirm out of your problems. For when your patience is finally in full bloom, then you will be ready for anything, strong in character, full and complete" (James 1:2-4).

God has a very special plan for your life. It began long ago when He first created you. He formed you lovingly, carefully, exactly to His specifications, every detail just as He wanted it—your looks, your abilities, your place of birth, the family you were to be born into (or the lack of it!). Nothing about you or your life has been accidental up to this point. In love He reached out and drew you to Himself through circumstances He had arranged just for that purpose. You were given a new birth, new life through His Holy Spirit when you accepted His Son, Jesus Christ, as your Savior, and were baptized, saturated with the Holy Spirit. And now God's plan is to make you full and complete!

"For because of our faith, he has brought us into this place of highest privilege where we now stand, and we confidently and joyfully look forward to *actually becoming* all that God has had in mind for us to be" (Rom. 5:2).

God wants us to *become* something.

Why of course, we all know that! God wants us to become more loving, more kind, more patient, have more faith, peace, gentleness, kindness, humility, and self-discipline, so that we can be His witnesses wherever we are! Isn't that true?

Sure it is, but most of us think that means we have to embark on a rigorous program of self-improvement, trying to make ourselves more loving, kind, patient, humble, gentle, and disciplined. And the harder we try, the more frustrated we become.

God has to do the changing. He wants us to commit ourselves to Him and trust that He will transform us.

"With eyes wide open to the mercies of God, I beg you, my brothers, as an act of intelligent worship, to give him your bodies, as a living sacrifice, consecrated to him, and acceptable by him. Don't let the world around you squeeze you into its own mold, but let God remold your minds from within, so that you may prove in practice that the plan of God for you is good, meets all His demands and moves toward the goal of true maturity" (Rom. 12:1-2 Phillips).

How does God bring about the changes in us? *How* does He break the old habit-patterns of thought and action we've lived with for years—characteristics we've called "personality-traits," or "personal likes and dislikes," or "preferences," or "strong opinions," that on closer examination, under the scrutiny of God's Holy Spirit of Truth, are seen to be part of the self-centered, defensive, selfish behavior that for years had separated us from the love of God and the love of others.

What methods does God use to change us?

"At present you are temporarily harassed by all kinds of trials and temptations. This is no accident—it happens to prove your faith, which is infinitely more valuable than gold . . . [which] must be purified by fire. This proving of your faith is planned to result in praise and honor and glory in the day when Jesus Christ reveals Himself" (I Pet. 1:6-7 Phillips).

So that is how our faith grows! And we read earlier how patience, endurance, and steadfastness grow when our life is full of difficulties, temptations, and problems.

I've heard some people say, "If that's the only way to get more patience and faith, I think I'd just as soon live with a little less of it!"

If that's the way you think, it is because you don't really trust God. Deep down you have your doubts about His plan and His love for you.

When God showed His prophet Jeremiah that he would have to go with the Jews into Babylonian captivity for a lifetime, God also said, "For I know the plans I have for you, says the Lord. They are plans for good and not for evil, to give you a future and a hope" (Jer. 29:11).

The years of suffering in Babylon were part of God's plan for Jeremiah and the Jews. It was a good plan, the best plan, designed to give them a future and a hope.

God's plan for you and for me is a good plan. Can you take His Word for that?

Why can't our faith grow in pleasant, easy circumstances? It does, as we come to trust and rely more and more on God's promises. But the purifying, the testing of our faith, has to come through circumstances that are a challenge to our determination to believe, trust, rely on God's word, *in spite of* what our senses tell us. For so long we've trusted our senses, our emotions, and our intellect to dictate our beliefs. We must be broken of that habit in order to exercise faith. Faith, remember, means a deliberate determination to believe something we can't see or feel the evidence of.

So if God tells us He's working everything out for our good, and we see everything go wrong, our faith grows when we stand on God's Word and thank Him for everything that happens.

How do you think Abraham's faith grew?

Would you have faith to walk up on a mountain with your only son, prepared to sacrifice him on the altar at God's command, and still believe that God was going to bless and multiply your descendants through that same son?

If you had been a friend of Abraham, could you have watched his crazy venture in faith and praised God, believing that even if Abraham was making a mistake, God would still work it out for good?

God alone can remake us, remold us from within. Our part is to follow Paul's advice to the Romans; to submit ourselves fully to Him, believe that He has taken over, and then accept eagerly and joyfully with thanksgiving and praise all the circumstances God uses to bring about His transformation of our lives.

There is the classic story of the pastor who prayed for more patience, and discovered the next day that his longtime efficient secretary had become ill. In her place was a volunteer who turned out to be the slowest office-worker the pastor had ever seen. He fussed and fumed in secret for a while, until he finally realized that the new secretary was an answer to his prayer. How else could he learn more patience? He began to thank and praise God for His choice of secretary and she soon improved remarkably.

Faith and patience are essential characteristics of a Christian life and witness; yet there is another quality we must have or else we've missed the point of the Good News.

"Let love be your greatest aim," Paul wrote to the Corinthians (I Cor. 14:1).

"Your strong love for each other will prove to the world that you are my disciples," said Jesus (John 13:25).

"This is My commandment, that you love one another [just] as I have loved you . . . that your joy . . . may be full," Jesus said (John 15:12, 11 *Amplified Bible*).

Love . . . love . . . love . . . As Christians we talk a great deal about it.

God is love, Jesus loves you, I love you. But we fall woefully short of really loving one another.

Jesus said, "I *demand* that you love each other as much as I love you" (John 15:12).

Love means more to us than anything else in the world. We were created to love God and to love one another. When we don't love, fearful things happen in us. We become hurt, resentful, afraid of each other, hateful, and guilt-ridden.

The wounds of our emotions, our fears and frustrations, our defense mechanisms, our destructive ways—all have come about for lack of love.

Educators, psychologists, sociologists, and all kinds of experts have told us what a difference love makes in the development of human beings.

A love that accepts, approves of, believes in others, is patient, kind, never selfish or envious, never proud or seeking its own reward or way, not touchy or irritable, doesn't hold grudges, and doesn't pay attention when it must suffer wrong. A love that is loyal, that believes the best and expects the best, is never glad when someone suffers wrong, but always happy when truth wins out. Such a love endures without weakening in all circumstances.

This is the kind of love God has for us, and the kind of love He commands that we have for each other. This is the kind of love that heals the wounds of old hurts, casts out old fears, melts away resentments and old grudges. This is the kind of love that makes us whole and able to love in return without fear of being rejected or hurt.

This is the love the Greeks called *agape,* a deliberate, reasoning, intentional, spiritual devotion. This is the love that is a fruit of the Holy Spirit, and when it is fully grown, it is the light that draws others to its source—God's love for us in Christ Jesus.

Every one of the gifts and manifestations of the Holy Spirit are given specifically to show God's love and concern for our every need. God heals because He loves; He performs miracles because He loves. God *is* love, and His power in us and through us is love—a supernatural, divine, intensely personal love for each individual in His creation.

His message to the world is one of love, and we are to be His messengers, the channels for His love. In order to accomplish this, His plan is to make *us* loving too.

But if love can only come to us from God, if it is a fruit of the Holy Spirit, how can Jesus command us to love? Mustn't we wait till He makes us more loving? Again we are faced with a promise in God's word that we must accept on faith.

Love is a fruit of the Spirit, and God's word says that the Holy Spirit dwells in us, therefore we can expect love to be present in our life. We have been given the ability to love, but we must step out on faith and choose to practice it.

Remember, *agape* is a deliberate, intentional love. We are told to love each other, even if we don't *feel* loving.

When we step out on faith, choosing to act on God's Word, then what happens? We know that our step of faith releases God's supernatural power of love, and this power begins to transform us, *making* us more loving, while the power also flows through us to the person we've deliberately *willed* to love.

How does that actually work in practice?

I had prayed for God to make me more loving, and had come to think of myself as a not too unloving sort of person. In fact as I traveled and ministered to thousands of people all of whom seemed to be blessed, I rejoiced that I was able to feel more love for others all the time.

Then one day I was faced with an individual so miserable and repulsive that I cringed at the sight and realized to my horror that I felt no love for this creature, but only wished that she would disappear as soon as possible.

She was a girl who had been brought to my office with her soldier boyfriend. Her face was caked with old makeup and dirt, her hair hung like strands of wire, and her clothes were filthy and torn. Her legs were scarred and smeared with dirt, and the odor from her body filled the room. The expression on her face was sullen and hateful, and her eyes were swollen from crying.

This poor creature had come to Fort Benning to tell the soldier that she was expecting his baby. The boy admitted that he was responsible for her condition, but had flatly refused to marry her. The girl had flown into a rage and threatened to kill him and then herself. She had already had another baby out of wedlock, and this time she was determined to either get married or die.

I looked at her and thought I had never seen anyone so unlovable, so desperate, so frightened, and so lonely. Yet, the very thought of praying for her was offensive to me. I didn't want to touch her.

"Lord," I cried inwardly, "why did you bring her to me?"

"She's one of my children," came the answer. "She is lost and in need of my love and healing. I brought her here for you to love her and tell her of my love."

The painful realization hit me suddenly. I had boasted to myself of being able to love, yet now I cringed at the sight of one who desperately needed to be loved.

"O, Lord," I cried inside, "forgive me, and thank you for showing me just how shallow and selfish my love is. Take my unlovingness and fill me with your love for her."

The girl was sobbing and her eyes looked dull behind the swollen lids smeared with mascara.

"Please, Sir," she said, "do something!"

"Do you believe in God?"

She nodded and whispered, "Yes, I do."

"Do you believe He can help you?"

She hesitated, then spoke slowly. "I know He *can* help me, but I don't think He'd want to. I used to be a Christian, but look at me now. Even if He wanted to help me, what could He do to get me out of this mess?"

"God *can* help you, and He *wants* to," I said with an assurance I didn't yet feel.

She shook her head and her shoulders sagged in utter hopelessness.

"Please," I said. "Try to understand that God loves you. He will fill you with His joy and peace and meet your every need before you leave my office today."

The girl stared, openmouthed, and the soldier looked as if he thought I was going to try to force him to marry the girl.

"God brought you here today," I continued. "He has permitted all the troubles in your life just so that you could understand how much He loves you. He has a wonderful plan for your life, and if you begin to trust Him and thank Him for everything that has happened to you, you will discover that God is helping you right now."

"Thank Him for this?" Her eyes blazed in sudden anger again. "All I want is for this man to marry me so my child will have a name."

"Look here." I showed her the underlined verse in my open Bible. "In every thing give thanks, for this is the will of God in Christ Jesus concerning you" (I Thess. 5:18 KJV). I flipped the pages to Rom. 8:28 (KJV). "All things work together for good to them that love God."

Her eyes stared in blank mistrust, and I suddenly realized how futile it was to speak to this wounded creature about God's love or any kind of love. She didn't know the meaning of the word. Only God could light the spark of understanding in her mind.

"May I pray for you?"

She nodded dully. "Sure, why not?"

I moved to place my hand on her head, and as I looked down I saw just how dirty and in need of a scrubbing she was. The twinge of revulsion made me shudder.

"Oh, Lord," I whispered, "how endless your love is for us—so much greater than the little love we are capable of on our own. Please, God, let your love touch her now, and teach me to love her."

51

Then I placed my hand firmly on her head and began to pray out loud.

"God, I know it is your will that we praise you in everything. Nothing in this world can happen without your will and permission. This dear child of yours has been hurt. She is sick, bruised, forsaken, and unloved by man, but I know you love her. Thank you for all that has brought her to this day in her life. Help her, Lord. I believe you are helping her to see your love and to praise you right now . . . "

I felt the girl begin to tremble under my hand. God was touching her with His love.

"Can you thank God for everything now?"

"Oh, yes," she burst out. "I thank you, God. I really do thank you for everything."

I continued to pray. "God, I believe you are healing this broken spirit. You are putting new life into her; you are giving her joy in the place of sorrow, victory in the place of defeat."

When I stepped back, her face shone with tears.

"What happened?" she exclaimed. "I feel so different! I'm not all churned up inside anymore; it's so quiet in me. I've never felt like this before. I'm happy; I really am!" Her eyes were wide with surprise. "What did it?"

"God has done it because we believed Him and praised Him," I said, suddenly realizing that something equally miraculous had happened in me. I stared at the girl, and she looked like a different person. I wanted to put my arms around her. She seemed so beautiful, so clean, so holy!

"Thank you, Lord." I felt my spirit soaring upward. "I *love* that girl. Thank you for changing *me,* Lord."

I could never have made myself more loving by trying to change my attitude toward the girl. God had to do the changing. My part was to admit and confess my own lack of love, then submit in faith to God's transforming power in willingness to love.

The harder we try to change ourselves, the more frustrated we become, and the more guilty we feel about our own shortcomings.

God brings certain people into our lives just to show us how incapable we are of loving others in our own strength. He doesn't do it to make us feel bad; He does it to give us an opportunity to experience His transforming love in our life and in the lives of the people He has called us to love.

Do you thank Him for the people in your life who are difficult to love? Do you have a cranky neighbor? A difficult boss? Praise God for them, because He loves you and wants to make your joy full by making it possible for you to love them. He loves them too, and wants to use you as a channel for His love to them.

I think perhaps the most wonderful and most challenging opportunities to love come in our own homes, right where we live. Does your husband or wife have certain qualities that rub you the wrong way? Are your parents difficult to live with? Your children rebellious?

Love one another, Jesus said. Accept one another; thank God for one another.

It isn't easy to thank God for an alcoholic husband or for an indifferent, rebellious child. It isn't easy to love someone who says he doesn't want our love.

It isn't easy to admit that beam in our eye, the self-righteousness, the self-pity, the role we've played as a long-suffering martyr. Can we thank God for bringing the people into our lives to show us the beam in our eye?

Can we thank God for them, just as they are, and especially for the things that make them hard to love? Can we confess our inability to love them *for* their irritating habits? Can we tell God we *want* to love them and then submit ourselves to Him to be remolded, remade, so that we can love them perfectly, according to His will and plan for us?

Then we can confidently expect God to work a miracle in us. It may happen instantaneously; we *feel* a wonderful spark of love, and of course we rejoice and praise the Lord for that. But watch out and don't become dependent on feelings. That first spark may die down, and we may sit around waiting for a second touch without doing anything in the meantime.

To love, deliberately and intentionally as Christ loves us, always requires the setting of our will. Whether we *feel* any love to begin with or not doesn't change the fact that we *do* love. God will show us practical and specific ways to communicate that love to the person He has placed in our life, and soon we will experience and sense a deeper love than any we've ever felt before. Our love will be stable and consistent, because it flows from a source beyond our own limited resources. It is God's love filling us to overflowing, spilling over to others through us. This is what it means to be rooted in God's love; and in that fertile soil, our own ability to love will grow and grow.

That is how the Holy Spirit bears fruit in our lives.

A Christian woman had been married to an alcoholic for many years until finally he got into trouble with the law and ended up in prison. The wife had struggled to raise their children on the meager welfare allowance they received from the state. Faithfully she had brought them to church and enjoyed the sympathy and respect of her community.

"Poor Edna," her friends would say. "She's raised those kids alone, never missed a Sunday in church, and never a word of complaint. While that good-for-nothing husband of hers never has been able to hold down a job, lying drunk most of the time to the disgrace and shame of his fine family . . . "

While her husband was in prison, Edna felt justified in getting a divorce. Now at last, she would be free to raise her children in a better environment.

One day a friend brought her a copy of *Prison to Praise.*

It seemed an almost impossible task to thank God for all the years of misery she had suffered, but she read how praise had changed the lives of others, and she decided to try it.

"Thank you for Al and his drinking," she prayed. "Thank you for the years of poverty and fear and loneliness."

Soon she heard that her former husband had been released from prison and had gone back to his old drinking habits. Still she continued to thank God for her circumstances.

Slowly she became aware of some things in her own life that she had never seen before. As she continued to thank God for her ex-husband, asking God to help her love him and accept him just as he was, she began to realize that for years she'd been guilty of something far more serious than drinking.

She'd been looking at the mote in her husband's eye and been totally unaware of the beam in her own. She had judged him for his drinking, feeling self-righteous and worthier than he was, and at the same time she'd lived each day steeped in self-pity, depression, and joyless martyrdom.

"Oh, Lord," she finally cried out one day, "I see that my sin has been so much graver than Al's. You gave us the commandment to love one another and to rejoice in our trials, and I didn't love or find any joy. Forgive me, Lord, and thank you for putting Al in my life so I could see myself. Now make it up to him. Heal the hurts he's suffered, and touch him with your love."

From that day on, Edna found it easy to rejoice in her circumstances. She *knew* God had brought them about as a part of His plan to fill her life with love and joy. As she continued to praise Him, all the old feelings of self-pity and depression rolled away; each day became a new, joyous experience, and she was aware of the presence of Jesus Christ in a new, exciting way.

Before long her former husband stumbled into a church service, accepted Christ as his Savior, and was completely healed of the alcoholism which had held him bound for fifteen years. Edna and Al remarried, and Al enrolled in college to start a brand-new life of serving God.

A difficult relationship or a trying set of circumstances may be God's loving way of providing us with an opportunity to grow, to exercise our spiritual muscle, or it may be His loving way of exposing a particular weakness or error in us.

Whatever the reason, we have grounds to rejoice. Any weakness, however well hidden, is like a crack in the foundation of a building.

"Therefore this iniquity and guilt shall be to you as a broken section of a high wall, bulging out and ready [at some distant day] to fall, whose crash will then come suddenly and swiftly, in an instant" (Isa. 30:13 *Amplified Bible*).

Sooner or later, a crack in the foundation will cause the entire building to fall down. The cracks we are aware of, we can do something about. We can confess all our known sins and weaknesses and be assured that once they are confessed, they are also forgiven, and God's love covers and heals the scars and the memories. But what about the hidden cracks, the hidden sins that come to the surface only as a vague sense of restlessness, insecurity, confusion, resentment, or any number of such symptoms we all know from experience?

The particular iniquity Isaiah was referring to in the verse above was the Israelites' repeated refusal to act on God's Word; instead, they sought the counsel of their own seers and human advisers. They preferred to rely on themselves instead of on God.

Self-reliance and self-assurance are always serious cracks in our foundation. If God brings us into circumstances that reveal an area of life where we've been relying on ourselves, shouldn't we thank Him for our helplessness and rejoice in the strength and power He can give us?

A young man in officer's training at Fort Benning, Georgia, found himself in circumstances he couldn't cope with.

"I need help, or I'll go out of my mind," he told me.

He had always been sure he could face every circumstance in life with success. His self-assurance bordered on cockiness. But since coming to officer candidate school, he had found himself unable to function as before, and his self-image and entire outlook on life was shattered.

The rigorous training for officer candidates is designed not only to teach the young men their duties as army officers, but is also meant to expose any weakness in the candidate that might endanger the lives of his men in combat. A certain stress is deliberately put on the candidates to test what "stuff" they are made of; if any are going to crack under pressure, it is better to find out before they are put in charge of troops.

The instructors had sensed that this particular candidate was unsure of himself under the mask of self-sufficiency he wore. The pressure had been put on. From early morning until late at night he was under surveillance. Every move he made was criticized.

"Can't you move faster, candidate?"

"Are you too dumb to follow instructions?"

"Do you always eat like a pig?"

"Don't you have any backbone?"

"Do you want your mother to help you?"

"Run around the building once more, candiate—maybe you'll learn to pick up your feet!"

The confidence the candidate had felt in himself was rapidly diminishing. Humiliated and helpless, he was at his wit's end, ready to desert the army and leave the country if necessary to get away from his persecutors.

As we talked, he told me that he'd never really believed in God, and the Bible had never made much sense to him. But if there was a God who could help him, he wanted to believe.

I shared with him what the Bible had to say about his circumstances, that God had a perfect plan for his life, that the trials he was going through were part of that plan, and that God would relieve all the tension and stress if he would only turn over the reins of his life to Him and thank Him for everything.

The candidate looked drawn; his face and eyes showed the strain and lack of sleep.

"I've never been in this kind of spot before." He shook his head. "I'm at the end of my rope, and now you're telling me that God placed me in this predicament?"

"Let's say that God allowed it to happen," I said. "I'm sure He would rather have had you turn to Him and accept His provisions for your life without having to go through all this suffering. But since you kept insisting you could handle your life without help, God chose the most direct, most loving way to show you that you needed Him."

I turned to Paul's second letter to the Corinthians and read, "We should like you, our brothers, to know something of what we went through in Asia. At that time we were completely overwhelmed; the burden was more than we could bear; in fact we told ourselves that this was the end. Yet we believe now that we had this experience of coming to the end of our tether that we might learn to trust, not in ourselves, but in God" (II Cor. 1:8-9 Phillips).

The candidate looked thoughtful, and agreed to let me pray for him, although he wasn't at all sure it would do any good.

I placed my hand on his head and began to praise God for the situation, asking God to give the young candidate a new understanding of His love and concern for every detail of his life. As I prayed, he began to tremble; then tears began to flow. After a while he began to laugh out loud.

"Praise you, God," he cried. "Thank you, God; I see you care; I believe you love me."

He turned to me, his face beaming.

"God really did bring me to officer candidate school, didn't He?" he said. "He knew this is where I'd find the answer. I feel like a new person."

And indeed he was. He accepted Christ as his Savior and went on to complete OCS with excellent standing.

The crisis point in his life had revealed a serious crack in his foundation. When he could acknowledge and thank God for His hand in the circumstances, the crack was healed.

Circumstances that rip out the walls of our own self-sufficiency are God's blessings in disguise. We can truly thank God for them and praise Him for every blow that removes more of the illusion that we have the ability to handle our own situation. The more we praise Him, the easier the transition will be. Our joy will increase, and the pain will hardly be noticeable. We'll also discover that the more trying the circumstances, the more we will realize the real strength and power of Christ dwelling and growing in us.

Each challenge, each trial or opportunity for growth makes us better equipped to be channels for His love and power.

A young girl was faced with a series of tragedies. Her mother and two of her brothers died. Her father remarried, divorced, and remarried again. The girl was failing in college, and drinking heavily. Then she heard about Jesus and accepted Him as her Savior. For a time she was filled with joy, and as she shared her story, others came to know Jesus Christ. Her life was going smoothly, and she thought all the hard times were over.

Then the troubles began to pile up. She was in two automobile accidents and was injured in both of them. Next, a tumor appeared on her neck and had to be removed by a painful operation. One day she drank a coke and became seriously ill—the coke had been spiked with drugs. On her way to school she was badly frightened by an attacker with a knife; another day a man came after her with a gun. Prowlers came to her house at night; one of them broke in and raped her. At last she was fired from her part-time job because her boss was certain that she must be doing something wrong to get herself into all that trouble.

Through it all the girl struggled to hold onto her faith. The hardest burden to bear was the mistrust and suspicion of the church people she knew.

Then someone placed a copy of *Prison to Praise* in her hand. She read it and caught new hope. Perhaps God had a reason for permitting all the trouble she was going through. She began thanking Him for each calamity that had come into her life, and as she did, joy replaced the fear that had been gripping her.

"I suddenly realized that God is all I have," she told me. "Other people may have security. I have only Him, and everything that has happened has made me see this more clearly."

This young lady now goes about with a new, radiant power to witness for her Savior. She has a deepened understanding and compassion for others who suffer as she did.

She had learned to trust that all the circumstances of her life were controlled by God's loving hand, and she could look at every new trial and say, "I know that God allowed it, so it must be for my good."

Another young woman lost her husband suddenly. They had no children, and she felt indescribably lonely. When she went to seek comfort and sympathy from her own family, they refused to speak to her, and behaved as if she didn't exist.

She couldn't understand this total rejection. Her family had never treated her like this before, and the anguish of being alone and unwanted was more than she could bear. Her body was in pain, she was unable to sleep, and she began to lose weight rapidly.

Day and night she cried alone in her house, until she began to lose track of time. She realized that her mind was slipping.

In despair she cried out, "God, are you there? Do you care about me?" She heard no answer and found no relief.

Then one day she saw *Prison to Praise* in a local bookstore. She read on the back cover that the author was an army chaplain and put the book back on the counter. Her husband had been in the army when he died, and she was afraid of a fresh flood of memories. She went home empty-handed, but the title of the little book stayed in her mind all day, and one thought persisted: *Read it! Read it!*

She'd never felt such an urge to read anything before, and puzzled by the sense of urgency, she went back to the bookstore and purchased the little volume.

At home she began to read, and soon her tears started flowing. At times she cried so hard she couldn't see to read, and at one point she realized that she had sunk to her knees on the floor and was still reading on.

She was certain that God was speaking directly to her through the book, yet the message was an incredible one. Was He actually telling her to thank Him that her husband was dead? How could God be so cruel? Everything in her seemed to rebel against the idea. Yet, as she read on, her sobs became more quiet and a new peace entered her heart. Slowly her thoughts began to take a new turn.

God has been in everything to help me she thought. *He knew that with my husband alive I would never have sought for Him! If my brother and his family had comforted me with kindness and love, I would have clung to them. Now I'm completely alone, and I'm coming to God. Oh Jesus, I feel your presence! You are here with me, and I praise and thank God for everything that brought me to you!*

The peace she felt in her heart was greater than anything she'd ever known before, and for the next several days her life radiated with a joy that completely astounded her friends and neighbors who had watched with growing concern how she had been broken down by grief.

Soon her brother came to see her with a tearful confession:

"Can you forgive me?" he said. "There's been a terrible misunderstanding. Someone told us that you had told your neighbor that we had refused to give you any help when your husband was dying. We were foolish enough to believe them and felt so shocked and hurt that we didn't want to see you or talk to you." The brother was overcome with shame. "Today we heard that the people had been talking about another widow! And to think that we left you alone when you needed us the most."

"Don't be sorry," the young widow cheerfully replied. "Be thankful you made the mistake!"

"What do you mean, Sis?" The brother was not sure he'd heard right. "I let you down when you really needed me; do you want me to thank God for that?"

"That's right," she laughed. "If you hadn't turned your back on me, I wouldn't have discovered just how much God loves me!"

The story is not meant to give an excuse for listening to gossip or for ignoring people who need our love. But God wants us to understand that when we trust our lives to Him, we can be sure that no one can treat us unfairly unless God allows it for our good. We can thank Him for every unkind word or sneaky, underhanded back-stabbing that comes our way.

"God will bless you for this, if you endure the pain of undeserved suffering because you are conscious of his will. For what credit is there in enduring the beatings you deserve for having done wrong? But if you endure suffering even when you have done right, God will bless you for it" (I Pet. 2:19-20 *Good News for Modern Man*).

A rosebush must be pruned to bear perfect roses. Jesus said, "I am the true Vine, and my Father is the Gardener. He lops off every branch that doesn't produce. And he prunes those branches that bear fruit for even larger crops. He has already tended you by pruning you back for greater strength and usefulness by means of the commands I gave you" (John 15:1-3).

These are the commands Jesus gave:

" 'Love the Lord your God with *all* your heart, soul, and mind.' This is the first and greatest commandment. The second most important is similar: 'Love your neighbor as much as you love yourself' " (Matt. 22:38-39).

The love Jesus spoke of was a deliberate love, one that required the setting of our will to love, a love exercised in faith. Jesus described the nature of this love when He said, "Love one another as I have loved you" (John 15:12 RSV).

Anything in us that prevents us from obeying that command must be pruned away. We're only delaying and hindering His work in us if we balk and complain about the painful pruning circumstances. These things don't come to us by accident or by the quirk of some cruel fate, but because our loving Father is our loving Gardener. We can rejoice and thank Him, because He knows what is best for us.

A Christian officer candidate at Fort Benning received word that his wife had been committed to a mental hospital after a severe breakdown. The doctors gave a poor prognosis for her recovery and said that she would have to be in the hospital for an indefinite time.

When John came into my office, he could not speak at first. I watched his tall frame shake with sobs as tears coursed down his grief-lined face.

"Why, oh, why did it happen?" He fought to utter the words. "My wife and I have tried to live good Christian lives; why has God deserted us now?"

"God hasn't deserted you," I said. "He has a real purpose in letting your wife go to the hospital. Why don't we kneel and thank Him for it?"

John stared at me. "Sir, I'm a Lutheran, and I've never read anything like that in my Bible!"

"What about this verse?" I suggested. "Always give thanks for everything to our God and Father in the name of our Lord Jesus Christ" (Eph. 5:20).

John shook his head. "I know that verse," he said. "I've always thought it meant to thank God for good things. Thanking Him for bad things just don't seem scriptural. I always thought Paul was a little extreme when he wrote about taking pleasure in infirmities."

"I used to think so, too," I said. "But I've become convinced that Paul is right. When he speaks about rejoicing in infirmities, he obviously doesn't mean we are supposed to find pain pleasurable in itself. But Paul had come to see his suffering from a different perspective. He had learned that his pain served a higher purpose and was part of God's loving plan for him."

John looked thoughtful. "I just don't know," he said slowly. "It doesn't make much sense."

"Paul learned his lesson the hard way, too," I went on. "Remember his 'thorn in the flesh'?"

John nodded.

"Three times Paul asked to have it removed. He was obviously not rejoicing in his pain right then. And three times God answered him, 'No. But I am with you; that is all you need. My power shows up best in weak people.' Now I am glad to boast about how weak I am; I am glad to be a living demonstration of Christ's power, instead of showing off my own power and abilities" (II Cor. 12:9).

"Paul wasn't happy about his infirmities for their own sake," I continued. "He went on to tell the Corinthians, 'Since I know it is all *for Christ's good,* I am quite happy about "the thorn," and about insults and hardships, persecutions and difficulties; for when I am weak, then I am strong—the less I have, the more I depend on him' " (II Cor. 12:10).

John leafed thoughtfully through his Bible.

"I have faith that God is working in all things," he said at last. "But the rejoicing part is really hard for me."

"If we say we have faith but can't rejoice, doesn't that mean we haven't really committed ourselves to trusting that God is doing what is best?" I suggested.

John sat in silence, then he nodded with determination.

"I believe you're right," he said. "I want to try it."

We knelt together, and John's tall frame shook with sobs as he prayed, "God, I know you love my wife more than I do. I believe you're working out a wonderful plan for us."

The tears were flowing freely down his face, but his eyes shone with a new confidence.

"God is doing the right thing, Chaplain," he said. "I know it."

A few days later John applied for compassionate transfer so that he could be near his wife. The request was eventually granted, and he came to say good-bye.

"Wait till you hear the best part," he said excitedly. "God has promised to heal my wife the moment I see her if I place my hands on her head and say, 'In Jesus name be healed.' "

I felt a twinge of doubt. What if John in his eagerness was jumping ahead of God? Then I, too, felt the assurance of the Holy Spirit, and placed my hand on John in a parting prayer.

"Father, you say that if two agree on earth concerning anything we ask for, you will do it for us (Matt. 18:19). So now I agree with John that the moment he touches his wife, you will heal her."

61

Two weeks later John's letter came.

"It happened just like Jesus told us it would. My wife was standing in the psychiatrist's office when I first saw her. She looked terrible. The lines in her face and the fear in her eyes almost convinced me she was beyond help. But I knew I had to obey what God had told me, and so I walked over and put my hands on her. The moment I touched her something like a shock went through her, and I knew she was healed. I told the psychiatrist that she was healed, and he looked at me as if he thought *I* needed to be admitted. But they called me the next day, and the psychiatrist said, "I don't know how to account for it, but your wife seems to be well!" My wife is home now, happier than she's ever been before. She has been strengthened by the afflictions she suffered, and she now joins me in being thankful for all things. We've learned how much of Christ's healing power is released when we praise Him."

God's strength can replace our weakness when we come to Him, recognizing and admitting where we fall short. But so often we're ashamed to confess that we are weak, afraid that others and God will not accept us as we really are. This kind of thinking is rooted in the wrong idea that we must earn or deserve God's love.

A Christian general came to me one day and confessed that the strain of presenting a perfect image before his men was about to kill him. As we talked, I realized that this man, whom I'd often admired for his outward poise and confidence, had never been able to accept himself as he really was. He was obsessed by the fear that if he should ever relax, he would grievously disappoint his family and his men.

I suggested that it would ease his tension if he would thank God for having created him exactly as he was.

"You mean, as I am today? Filled with fear and tension?" he asked, and I nodded.

"Do you think the God who created this universe and placed the stars in the heavens was any less careful when He created you? Nor has He been careless with the circumstances He has allowed into your life in order to show you how much He loves you."

The general came to several sessions in my office, and studied his Bible and read *Prison to Praise* with interest. Gradually he came to accept that God had a perfect plan for his life and that the continuous stress he'd felt was serving the purpose of bringing him to trust God.

He began to praise God for his anxieties, and a sense of peace slowly replaced the old habits of fear. For the first time in his life he was happy to be himself.

"As long as I thought that God couldn't love me with my weaknesses, I tried to hide them and consequently drifted farther and farther from the truth," he told me. "As soon as I was able to admit that I was weak, and thank God for having made me that way, His love began to transform me, and He began to fill me with His peace."

David wrote:

"Let everyone bless God and sing his praises, for he holds our lives in his hands. And he holds our feet to the path. You have purified us with fire, O Lord, like silver in a crucible. You captured us in your net and laid great burdens on our backs. You sent troops to ride across our broken bodies. We went through fire and blood. But in the end you brought us into wealth and great abundance... For I cried to him for help, with praises ready on my tongue. He would not have listened if I had not confessed my sins. But He listened! He heard my prayer! He paid attention to it! Sing to the Lord, all the earth! Sing of His glorious name!" (Psa. 66:8-12, 17-19, 1-2).

David wanted oneness with God, and he knew that anything unclean in him would prevent God's love from filling him and flowing through him. Therefore David welcomed the purifying, the breaking and cleansing process God put him through. He rejoiced when the trials revealed the hidden sins of his own heart, sins he could confess and be healed of. God Himself had shown David the way.

"I don't need your sacrifices of flesh and blood. What I want from you is your true thanks... *I want you to trust me in your times of trouble, so I can rescue you, and you can give me glory!* ... Recite my laws no longer, and stop claiming my promises, for you have refused my discipline, disregarding my laws. ... This is the last chance. ... But true praise is a worthy sacrifice; this really honors me. Those who walk my paths will receive salvation from the Lord" (Psa. 50:13-17, 22-23).

The paths of God are the paths of praise!

5

When Sparrows Fall

"Not one sparrow (What do they cost? Two for a penny?) can fall to the ground without your Father knowing it. And the very hairs of your head are all numbered. So don't worry! You are more valuable to him than many sparrows" (Matt. 10:29-31).

Jesus told his disciples that our Father in heaven keeps an eye on every sparrow and counts every hair on our heads; yet the fact remains that sparrows *do* fall. Tragedies *do* come to us. Innocent little children die under the wheels of cars driven by drunks. Someone we love is struck by cancer and dies in spite of our fervent prayers.

Could God have prevented the sparrow's fall? The tragedy? The child's death? The spread of cancer?

Most of us believe that God has the power to prevent such things *if* He wants to. We are then left to wrestle in our minds with the problem of *why* God permits what seems to us to be the triumph of evil over good.

Sometimes we draw the conclusion that God is calloused, uncaring, or partial; or we think that the victims of evil suffer because of their own or someone else's sin. Both conclusions are in stark contrast with the Good News of the Bible that tells us God is love, and we don't have to be good to deserve His loving care.

It is impossible to praise God for *all* things if we think that He is not really responsible for everything that happens, or that He is sometimes indifferent to suffering.

Often I receive letters from people who ask me if it is right to thank God for something that is evil, when the Bible tells us to hate evil. They quote, "Ye that love the Lord, hate evil" (Psa. 97:10 KJV) and "Hate the evil, and love the good" (Amos 5:15 KJV).

What is meant here is that we are not to approve of evil, practice evil, embrace evil, or submit to evil.

Praising God for evil circumstances does *not* mean that we approve of evil or accept evil for evil's own sake, except in the sense that Paul spoke of taking pleasure in pain—not for the sake of pain itself, but because we *know* that God is at work in and through it.

God did not create evil, because God is love. But God created beings with free will and the capacity for evil. Evil came about as a consequence of man's rebellion, and it remains in this world with God's permission, but is always subject to His will. Nothing evil can come near us without God's permission.

Because evil does exist, God sent His Son to die on the cross to break the power of evil in the lives of all who would believe in Him.

"The evil bow before the good," says Prov. 14:19 (KJV).

We who believe have been given the power to overcome the world.

"Every one who believes . . . that Jesus is the Christ . . . is a born-again child of God. . . . whatever is born of God is victorious over the world; and this is the victory that conquers the world, even our faith" (I John 5:1, 4 *Amplified Bible*).

So what is this faith to be grounded on? What are we to believe in order to overcome? We believe in Jesus Christ, but there is more to the package. To fully believe in Jesus Christ also means that we accept that God is the all-powerful God He says He is and that nothing happens without His knowledge or outside His will.

If we set ourselves to firmly believe this, and so praise God for every circumstance of apparent evil around us, I am convinced that *every* difficult situation, *every* tragedy, will be changed by the hand of God.

When I say this, I know that most of you will jump to the conclusion that God is going to change a situation to what *we* think is good. But that is *not* what I am saying.

When we fully trust an evil situation or condition to God, thanking and praising Him for it, the power of God will change, override, or overcome the intention and plan of the evil power inherent in the situation, transforming it to fit in with the *original,* perfect intention and plan of God.

We may not understand God's plan or recognize it as good, but when we praise Him for it, we release His power to work in the situation for our good.

(Our ideas of good and bad are often sadly distorted. For instance, if a child inherits a million dollars, we say, "How wonderful!" But if a child dies and goes home to heaven, we say, "How tragic!" Yet we know that a million-dollar inheritance can lead to tragedies, while going home to heaven can only be good.)

If we praise God in all circumstances, I believe that some sparrows will be prevented from falling, some little children will not die, some cancers will be halted and leave. Yet this is *not* to be our motivation for praising God. Some sparrows will still fall, some children will die, and some people will succumb to cancer. Our praise must be *for* these instances also.

We are told to praise God for bringing evil into our lives, trusting that He has a plan and purpose with it, but what are we supposed to do next? How do we personally react to evil when we come face-to-face with it. There is a lot of fuzzy thinking on this point among Christians.

Jesus told his followers, "Resist not evil" (Matt. 5:39). Yet we read that when He saw merchants selling cattle, sheep, and doves and exchanging money in the temple area, He "made a whip from some ropes and chased them all out, and drove out the sheep and oxen, scattering the money changers' coins over the floor and turning over their tables!" (John 2:15).

Here we see Jesus taking overt action against evil. Yet He did not resist the men who came to arrest Him in the Garden of Gethsemane, and He reprimanded the disciple who tried to defend Him with a sword.

So there is a time that God would lead us to take overt action against a force of evil; other times He would have us submit without resistance. How do we know when to do what?

I think our only recourse here is to recognize that in ourselves we have no power to overcome evil. The overcoming power is always God. The essence of God's message to us is that we must learn to focus our attention on Him, the source of overcoming power, and not direct our attention toward the evil confronting us. He will then direct our action moment by moment.

Paul told the Romans, "Do not let yourself be overcome by evil, but overcome (master) evil with good" (Rom. 12:21 *Amplified Bible*).

In the case of Jesus' arrest and crucifixion, it was His very act of nonresistance to evil that broke the power over evil in the world.

Jesus was showing us that there is a better way to deal with evil than to resist it in the sense that we think of resistance. Our idea of resistance is to react in kind, using force against force, and so we react to the evil circumstances opposing us, rather than responding to God's presence and guidance in the situation.

Anytime our action is prompted by the evil circumstances surrounding us rather than by our faith in God's power and perfect control of the situation, we're allowing evil to overcome us, rather than overcoming evil with the power of God.

Jesus was not a pacifist. When He said, "Resist not evil," He meant that we should instead *actively* recognize the power of God over evil and recognize that God sometimes chooses to use apparently evil circumstances to bring about His plan of good.

In such a case, to resist evil would mean that we were working to thwart God's perfect plan. If the disciples had succeeded in preventing the arrest of Jesus in the Garden of Gethsemane, they would have meddled in God's plan, although it would have seemed to them that they were scoring a victory over evil.

Jesus came to conquer, not to teach us how to lose without whimpering.

Both James and Peter tell us to stand firm in faith against Satan. If we look at the context of their message, it is clear that they are in complete agreement with Jesus and with Paul.

"So give yourself humbly to God. Resist the devil and he will flee from you. And when you draw close to God, God will draw close to you" (James 4:7). "Be careful—watch out for attacks from Satan, your great enemy. . . . Stand firm when he attacks. Trust the Lord. . . ." (I Pet. 5:8-9).

Our only defense against the power of Satan is the power of God. That power is released when we stand firm in our faith that God is in perfect and loving control of every detail of the circumstances surrounding us. We express that faith in praising and thanking Him for the situation.

We are told to be careful and watch for the enemy's attack, but our attention must be focused on God, not on Satan. We are to be aware of our enemy, but our protection doesn't lie in watching the enemy, but rather in our knowledge of God's power.

If we let fear and doubts and a preoccupation with the presence of evil take over our minds, we block the power of God from entering the situation. We must learn to see evil in the right perspective—subject to the mighty power of God—and then let that power work everything for good according to God's perfect plan.

Our part is to stand firm in faith, obedient to the promptings of the Holy Spirit, who will guide our outward actions in the situation. Inwardly, our part is *always* to keep our eyes on God and to praise and thank Him for His goodness and mercy in all things.

Standing firm in *faith* means that we must set our will to decide to accept God's Word that He is in charge, regardless of what our feelings or outward circumstances may be like.

The Bible firmly states that God is in charge of every rainstorm, earthquake, tornado or hurricane, every war, famine and pestilence, every birth or death, every flower in the field, every sparrow, and every hair on our heads. We will have to decide whether or not to believe Him all the way.

Some people say, "I can see that God is responsible for some things, but I can't accept that He is in charge of everything."

This is not an adequate basis for praise, and in the particular areas where we refuse to see God's hand, we can never expect to see an answered prayer or evidence of His transforming power.

Let us see what the Bible has to say about some areas where we have difficulty recognizing the hand of God.

Habakkuk was a prophet who complained about the conditions of his country much like some of us complain about the world today.

"O Lord, how long must I call for help before you will listen?" Habakkuk cried. (He didn't even think God was listening, and I'm afraid there are modern-day Christians who agree with him.) "I shout to you in vain; there is no answer. 'Help! Murder!' I cry, but no one comes to save. Must I forever see this sin and sadness all around me? Wherever I look there is oppression and bribery and men who love to argue and to fight. The law is not enforced and there is no justice given in the courts, for the wicked far outnumber the righteous, and bribes and trickery prevail" (Hab. 1:2-4).

Have you ever looked at twentieth-century America and voiced those thoughts? I have.

God answered the prophet, "Look, and be amazed! You will be astounded at what I am about to do! For I am going to do something in your own lifetime that you will have to see to believe. I am raising a new force on the world scene, the Chaldeans, a cruel and violent nation who will march across the world and conquer it!" (Hab. 1:5-6).

God said that *He* would raise up a cruel and violent nation to conquer the world. Do you think that any of the armies we've seen rise on the world scene since then came up any other way?

God didn't just *allow* the Chaldeans to conquer, He *raised* them up. What about Napoleon? Hitler? What about the Communist armies of Russia and China? Are we willing to thank God for raising them up? Can we accept His word that He is doing it for our good? Can we honestly praise Him for it?

Habakkuk was shocked when he heard what God intended to do.

"O Lord my God, my Holy One," he cried, "you who are eternal—is your plan in all of this to wipe us out? Surely not! O God our Rock, you have decreed the rise of these Chaldeans to chasten and correct us for our awful sins. We are wicked, but they far more. Will you, who cannot allow sin in any form, stand idly by while they swallow us up? Should You be silent while the wicked destroy those who are better than they?" (Hab. 1:12-13).

Have you ever wondered why God allowed evil and cruel men to hurt innocent ones? I have.

Habakkuk continued, "Are we but fish, to be caught and killed? . . . Must we be strung up on their hooks and dragged out in their nets, while they rejoice? . . . Will you let them get away with this forever?" (Hab. 1:14-15, 17).

God didn't turn a deaf ear to Habakkuk's questions, but told him to write down the answer for all the world to see and remember.

"These things I plan won't happen right away. Slowly, steadily, surely, the time approaches when the vision will be fulfilled. If it seems slow, do not despair, for these things will surely come to pass. Just be patient! They will not be overdue a single day!" (Hab. 2:3).

God is never late! His timing is perfect, but we are always fussing because our estimates are wrong.

"Not this," God told Habakkuk: "Wicked men trust themselves alone [as these Chaldeans do], and fail; but the righteous man trusts in me, and lives" (Hab. 2:4).

The Chaldeans would fail in the end; they would be betrayed by their own arrogance, carried away by their own greed. Their apparent glory would turn to shame, as the consequences of their evil would catch up with them until the time would come that all the earth would be filled with an awareness of the glory of God.

Now Habakkuk saw the greatness of God's plan, and he cried out in triumph, singing to God.

"O Lord, now I have heard your report, and I worship you in awe for the fearful things you are going to do. . . I see God moving across the deserts. . . His brilliant splendor fills the earth and sky; his glory fills the heavens, and the earth is full of his praise! What a wonderful God he is! From his hands flash rays of brilliant light. He rejoices in his awesome power. Pestilence marches before him; plague follows close behind. He stops; he stands still for a moment, gazing at the earth. Then he shakes the nations, scattering the everlasting mountains and leveling the hills. His power is just the same as always!" (Hab. 3:2-6).

Habakkuk was awed by the vision he had seen. He no longer questioned God's control over the fires, earthquakes, pestilence, famines, and wars. Habakkuk's lips quivered with fear, his legs gave way under him and he was shaking in terror, but he sang to God, "Even though the fig trees are all destroyed, and there is neither blossom left nor fruit, and though the olive crops all fail, and the fields lie barren; even if the flocks die in the fields and the cattle barns are empty, yet I will rejoice in the Lord; I will be happy in the God of my salvation. The Lord God is my Strength, and he will give me the speed of a deer and bring me safely over the mountains" (Hab. 3:17-19).

Habakkuk trembled in terror at the vision God had shown him of the future, but he also realized that God was a God of love, justice, and mercy, and he didn't hesitate to trust himself completely into His hands, praising Him for His perfect plan for Israel.

God's command to us is that we praise Him, too—even if our lips tremble in fear and we shake in terror over the outward circumstances of His plan for us.

Through the prophet Isaiah, God told His people that He intended to raise up King Cyrus of Persia to conquer and crush many nations. King Cyrus didn't know God, but God intended to use him to bring the Jewish captives home from Babylon and rebuild the temple and Jerusalem.

Why would God choose Cyrus, a heathen king, to carry out His purposes? To those who would question Him, God answered, "I form the light and make the dark. I send good times and bad. I, Jehovah, am he who does these things. . . . Woe to the man who fights with his Creator. Does the pot argue with its maker? Does the clay dispute with him who forms it, saying, 'Stop, you're doing it wrong!' or the pot exclaim, 'How clumsy can you be'? . . . Jehovah, the Holy One of Israel, Israel's Creator, says: What right have you to question what I do? Who are you to command me concerning the work of my hands? I have made the earth and created man upon it. With my hands I have stretched out the heavens and commanded all the vast myriads of stars. I have raised up Cyrus to fulfill my righteous purpose, and I will direct all his paths . . . " (Isa. 45:7, 9, 11-13).

When we refuse to see God's hand in every situation around us, we are like the pot arguing with its maker. We say, "Now if *I* was God, I certainly wouldn't do it *that* way. I wouldn't send an earthquake to Peru or let that little girl die of leukemia or allow that preacher to thunder untruth from the pulpit, leading gullible people astray . . . and I certainly wouldn't allow heroin-pushers to tempt little children!"

God knows how we feel about these things and how limited our understanding is. He spoke through the prophet Isaiah:

"This plan of mine is not what you would work out, neither are my thoughts the same as yours! For just as the heavens are higher than the earth, so are my ways higher than yours, and my thoughts than yours. As the rain and snow come down from heaven and stay upon the ground to water the earth, and cause the grain to grow and to produce seed for the farmer and bread for the hungry, so also is my Word. I send it out and it always produces fruit. It shall accomplish all I want it to, and prosper everywhere I send it" (Isa. 55:8-11).

Our skepticism and disappointment in God's plan is rooted in a distrust of God. We're not convinced that He has our best interest in mind.

We question why it is necessary for an innocent child to die under the wheels of a car driven by a drunk in order that the driver come to recognize his need for God. Does God care more for the soul of the drunken driver than He does for the child or the child's grieving parents?

We all ask countless questions like that, turning them over and over in our minds, and while we are torn by the questions, we have no peace and the situation remains unchanged.

The only way out of our dilemma is to accept God's Word on faith. Faith, in spite of what we think, feel, or see. His Word is that He loves us, and that the death of an innocent child *does* fit into God's loving plan for each of the lives affected.

God's love for us can be accepted only on faith, just as we accept every other promise in the Bible. We must decide to believe in the nature of His love, because He says it is so, regardless of whether we *feel* loved or not.

The Good News of the Bible is that God loves us with a love more kind, more patient, more long-suffering and concerned with our happiness and well-being than any human love can be. God loves us and has a perfect plan for our lives. He sent His Son to die for us, to provide us with a new life full of abundant joy and peace, in a world filled with suffering.

We can't possibly understand, with our limited human understanding, the magnificent scope of God's plan for us and for this world. Like Habakkuk, we are shocked that God intends to use earthquakes and wars, suffering and death to bring His plan about.

But God's plan is a perfect plan. It is the only plan that has ever worked on this earth where mankind's rebellion and evil has prevailed. Look at the bloody mess we've made in trying to order our own lives throughout history.

God's plan is not what we would work out, He told Isaiah, because His thoughts are so much higher than ours, His perspective so much higher.

God wants only what is best for us.

"You will live in joy and peace. The mountains and hills, the trees of the field—all the world around you—will rejoice. Where once were thorns, fir trees will grow; where briars grew, the myrtle trees will sprout up. This miracle will make the Lord's name very great and be an everlasting sign [of God's power and love]" (Isa. 55:12-13).

God wants to shower us with blessings. He wants to take care of us in every way, down to every little detail of our daily lives. Yet we insist on looking at all the circumstances, the outward workings of His plan, and speculate on what they mean and how they all fit in, while His command to us is that we look to Him and trust Him.

71

We make our understanding into a wall between us and God as long as we insist on figuring out and approving His plan before we dare trust ourselves to Him.

Here, just as in our first approach to God, acceptance of His will and plan must come before understanding. We must deliberately set aside our own desire for knowledge and comprehension of what God is doing, and throw the weight of our will into a decision to trust His Word.

His plan for us is good. Can we trust His Word for that?

His plan for Job was good, but it was a plan that tested Job's faith to the utmost and staggered his understanding.

Job was a good man. In fact, God said of him, "He is the finest man in all the earth—a good man who fears God and will have nothing to do with evil" (Job 1:8).

So what happened to Job? He lost everything he had. His cattle, his crops . . . and one day the roof fell in and killed all his children.

If that happened to you or to one of your neighbors, would you say it was God? Or Satan?

In Job's case it *was* Satan. But how did it come about? Satan came to God and asked His permission to bring the troubles on Job.

Satan may be the actor who acts out his role in the drama of our life, but God is still the Director.

So what was Job's response? He fell down on the ground before God and tore his clothes in grief.

"I came naked from my mother's womb . . . and I shall have nothing when I die. The Lord gave me everything I had, and they were His to take away. *Blessed be the name of the Lord!"* (Job 1:21).

But that wasn't the end of Job's troubles. Satan came and asked permission once more to torment Job, and God gave it.

This time Job was struck with boils all over his body, until he became so disfigured that no one could bear to look at him. His own wife told him to curse God and die, and his neighbors, who had always respected him, now mocked him and turned away. Three of his best friends, who came to tell him that his suffering was caused by his sins, advised him to repent.

Job never doubted that God had brought his misfortune. He cried out for mercy, but was convinced that it was not his sins that had brought about his suffering. Job knew in his heart that he was a righteous man, and he trusted God.

"Though he slay me, yet will I trust in him: I am going to argue my case with him" (Job 13:15 KJV and *Living Bible*).

Job's faith that God was in charge never wavered, but his understanding questioned God's purpose and methods. Job's questions have been echoed by all of us, at one time or another.

"Why do you allow poverty, God? Why do you allow the innocent to suffer? Why are evil men living in ease and comfort? Why don't you listen to my plea? God, why don't you let me die so my sufferings will end and I can rest with you?"

When God answered Job, it was the stern rebuke of a Father to a son.

"Where were you when I laid the foundations of the earth? Tell me, if you know so much. . . . Have you ever commanded the morning to appear, and caused the dawn to rise in the east? . . . Where is the path to the distribution point of light? Where is the home of the east wind? . . . Can you hold back the stars? . . . Can you ensure the proper sequence of the seasons? . . . Who gives intuition and instinct? Who makes the wild donkeys wild? . . . Have you given the horse strength, or clothed his neck with a quivering mane? . . . Is it at your command that the eagle rises high upon the cliffs to make her nest? . . . Do you still want to argue with the Almighty? Or will you yield? Do you—God's critic—have the answers?" (Job 38:4, 12, 24, 31-32, 36; 39:5, 19, 27; 40:2).

Job replied, "I am nothing—how could I ever find the answers? I lay my hand upon my mouth in silence. I have said too much already" (Job 40:4-5).

God continued His impressive list of His creation: the animals, their ways and strengths, God's power over all men.

"Who can stand before me? I owe no one anything. Everything under the heaven is mine!" (Job 41:10-11).

Job replied, "I know that You can do all things and that no thought or purpose of Yours can be restrained or thwarted. . . . I was talking about things I knew nothing about and did not understand, things far too wonderful for me. . . . I had heard of You only by the hearing of the ear; but now my [spiritual] eye sees You. . . . I loathe myself and repent in dust and ashes" (Job 42:2-3, 5-6 *Amplified Bible* and *Living Bible*).

The Lord spoke harshly also to Job's three friends who had totally misunderstood the reasons for Job's suffering. God told them they had been wrong and instructed them to offer up a burnt offering and then have Job pray for them.

The three men did as they were told, and "when Job prayed for his friends, the Lord restored his wealth and happiness! In fact, the Lord gave him twice as much as before" (Job 42:10).

It is interesting to note that God blessed Job when Job had blessed those who had accused him wrongly. Job had learned his lesson. No longer would he question God's operation of the universe. No longer would he see or hear with his natural senses only, but with his new, spiritual insight.

God had a perfect plan for Job. His trials were executed by Satan, but permitted by God to give Job greater faith and wisdom, and to show him just how great and loving God is.

God had a perfect plan for Ruth, the Moabite. Yet it looked for all the world as if misfortune followed her. First she lost her husband. Then she went with her mother-in-law back to Bethlehem and they were so poor that Ruth had to go into the fields of the rich farmers and glean whatever was left after the harvest. That doesn't sound like the outworking of a wonderful plan, does it? But Ruth trusted God, and there in the field she met Boaz, a rich relative of her dead husband. Boaz fell in love with Ruth and they were married. God's plan had worked, and Ruth became the grandmother of King David.

Or what about God's perfect plan for Joseph? God planned that Joseph would become Pharaoh's right-hand man in Egypt, because God intended to use him, at just the right time, to save the nation of Israel from famine.

Joseph was sold by his brothers as a slave to a caravan of merchants on their way to Egypt. It was the first step in God's plan, but Joseph's brothers had no idea that they were serving God's purpose. They hated their brother and meant only to harm him.

Later Joseph became the trusted servant of an influential Egyptian, and it looked as if he was on his way up the social ladder. But he was falsely accused of attempting to rape the Egyptian's wife and was thrown in jail. If that happened to you, would you think that the devil had won a victory? Or would you have accepted it as part of God's perfect plan?

It was in jail that God arranged for Joseph to meet Pharaoh's butler and interpret his dream. Joseph asked the butler to plead with Pharaoh to pardon him, and the butler promised, but forgot all about it. Joseph spent another two years in jail, and that surely looked like an unfortunate quirk of fate. But God's timing was perfect. Paraoh dreamed a strange pair of dreams that no one could interpret. Suddenly the forgetful butler remembered the fellow he'd met in jail a couple of years before. Joseph was brought before Paraoh, and God told Joseph the meaning of Pharaoh's dreams. Seven years of bountiful harvests would be followed by seven years of severe famine. Pharaoh accepted the interpretation of his dreams, and appointed Joseph to be in charge of the ingathering and storage of grain during the seven rich years, and in charge of the distribution of food during the seven lean years to follow.

When Joseph's brothers came to Egypt to buy grain, he revealed his identity, and they fell down before him, stricken with fear and remorse. But Joseph said, "Don't be angry with yourselves that you did this to me [sold me into slavery], for God did it! He sent me here ahead of you to preserve your lives. . . . It was God who sent me here, not you! . . . As for you, you thought evil against me; but God meant it for good, to bring about that many people should be kept alive, as they are this day" (Gen. 45:5, 8; 50:20 *Amplified Bible* and *Living Bible*).

God *meant* it for good! We often will admit that God is able to make all things work out to good for us, the way the Bible says, but we think that God takes whatever happens to us and makes the best of it, sort of a secondhand blessing. But God isn't on the defensive. He isn't limited to making the best out of a bad situation. *God has the initiative!* We need to remind ourselves of that ever so often.

God had the initiative when Stephen was stoned to death (Acts 7). Stephen was a man, full of the Holy Spirit, who served the Lord faithfully. When he was stoned to death, Saul of Tarsus, an angry young persecutor of Christians, was among the spectators.

Stephen obviously trusted that God was completely in charge of the situation, for he knelt down while the stones were being hurled at him, and cried out with a loud voice, "Lord, don't charge them with this sin!" And then he died. Stephen knew that although his persecutors meant evil against him, God meant it for good.

Would you be able to thank God for the murder of the most Christlike Christian man you know and believe He was using the seeming tragedy for some great good?

Saul of Tarsus became Paul the apostle after a remarkable conversion experience on the road to Damascus. He experienced his share of what looked like mishaps in spreading the gospel.

Once when Paul and Silas came to Philippi, they were accused of corrupting the city and were stripped and beaten with wooden whips until the blood ran from their bare backs. Then they were put in the inner dungeon of the prison with their feet clamped in stocks (Acts 16:20-24).

But Paul and Silas didn't think that Satan had won a victory or that God had deserted them. They were convinced that God had called them to preach in Philippi, and that He was working in everything to bring about His perfect plan for them. So they didn't whine or complain or cry out to the Lord for help. They sat there in the dungeon with the blood stiffened on their sore backs, unable to stretch their aching legs, and they were praying and singing hymns of praise to God.

Suddenly, at midnight, there was a great earthquake, the prison doors flew open, and the chains fell off every prisoner. The jailer was horrified, thinking they had all escaped, and drew his sword to kill himself. But Paul yelled out, assuring him that all the prisoners were there, and the jailer came and threw himself down before their feet. "What must I do to be saved?" he begged.

Beginning with the jailer and his entire family, the people of Philippi received the Gospel (Acts 16).

God had a perfect plan for the city of Philippi. He sent Paul and Silas to be His witnesses there, and they had faith to believe that God was working out His plan, even if He used circumstances they could not have anticipated.

We are always trying to anticipate what God will do. Because He worked out a set of circumstances one way once, we draw the conclusion that He will do the same thing in every similar set of circumstances. But Paul wasn't always dramatically released from prison. Sometimes he stayed there for years.

Paul suffered many afflictions. He was stoned and left for dead, shipwrecked, bitten by a snake, suffered disease and persecution . . . but never once did he think that God had stopped directing every incident of his life. He counted it all for joy and an opportunity to praise God. Paul knew that his suffering was working *for* him.

For years I suffered with excruciating headaches. In vain I searched the Scriptures, clinging to God's promise of healing, but I couldn't find a clue to the reason for my agony, nor did it go away.

In the meantime, I was tormented with doubts. Over and over I allowed myself to speculate *why* this particular suffering had come my way. The thoughts whirled in my head. *"Why doesn't God do something about your pain? You're praying for others who get healed, but your own pain is still with you.*

As I suffered and tossed through long, sleepless nights, the thoughts persisted. *Look how miserable you are! If God is a just God who knows about your suffering, He surely wouldn't hold it against you if you ended your life. Just be careful how you do it, and no one will suspect suicide; no one will be hurt, and you'll be free from the pain . . .*

Like the arguments of Job's friends, these thoughts can sound very reasonable when you are racked with pain. But of course, they are a bunch of lies, invented by the master deceiver, Satan himself, who comes near only by permission of God.

Our accuser and tormentor must flee when we draw near to God and take our stand on His Word of truth.

My headaches didn't suddenly go away, but I determined to believe that God wouldn't permit anything to happen to me unless it was for my good. Therefore, the headaches had to be for my good, and I began to praise and thank God for them every time they came. As I did, something wonderful began to happen inside me. Strange as it may seem, my pain began to work *for* me. The more I hurt, the more thankful I became, and with the thanksgiving I experienced a new depth of joy radiating through my entire being.

Richard Wurmbrand tells what happened when the physical pain and mental agony of a Communist prison became more than he could bear. Three years of solitary confinement and torture was threatening to rob him of his sanity, but as he reached the extremity of his endurance, Richard Wurmbrand still trusted God and praised Him for His ever-present mercy and love. Wurmbrand tells how, at this point, joy began to radiate through his being, filling his cell.

God meant his suffering for good. Richard Wurmbrand's ministry is now influencing the entire world *because* of what he suffered.

"As for God, his way is perfect," said the psalmist: "the word of the Lord is tried: he is a buckler to all those that trust in him" (Psa. 18:30 KJV).

The way may lead through fierce battles, through raging storms, or fire or flood; yet everywhere, God's presence goes with us, and His hand guides us, says the Bible.

How can we doubt it? He created the soldier and his weapons, the storm, the fire, and the waters of the flood. They are all under His perfect control.

Why did God cause a storm on the lake when Jesus was there in a boat with His disciples? Only so that His power and authority over the storm could be demonstrated (Mark 4).

Why did God cause a man to be blind from birth?

Jesus and His disciples were walking along when they saw a man blind from birth. " 'Master,' his disciples asked him, 'why was this man born blind? Was it a result of his own sins or those of his parents?' 'Neither,' Jesus answered. 'But to demonstrate the power of God.' " Then Jesus went on to heal the man (John 9:2-3).

The disciples looked at the blind man from the viewpoint of human reasoning and understanding; Jesus saw the situation under the perfect control and power of God.

Our viewpoint makes all the difference.

I've received hundreds of letters from people who've read *Prison to Praise.* Seventy-five percent of the letters come from people who tell me how they've started praising God for a difficult situation, with amazing results. Twenty-five percent of the letters come from people who tell of the same kinds of situations, but they are not able to believe that God is at work and can't praise Him for it. They are defeated, discouraged, and desperate.

The difference is not in the situation, but in the viewpoint, and consequently in the outcome.

Many write about the death of a close friend or relative.

"Tom suffered so terrible," wrote one lady. "We had taken him to healing services and prayer groups all over the country. He seemed better for a while, and our hopes soared. Then the cancer came back, and after months of agony he died. How could God be so inconsistent? I can't believe it was His will that Tom die so young. He was a Christian and wanted to serve God. If God did it all just to teach the rest of us a lesson, why did Tom have to suffer? I can't believe I'm supposed to praise God for what has happened."

Here is another letter:

"Charles accepted Christ less than a year ago. He was a radiant witness for the Lord. After six months he developed cancer. He had two operations, but the growth in his lungs returned. He called the elders of his church; they anointed him and prayed for his healing. When he went back for his checkup, the growth had disappeared. Charles rejoiced and praised the Lord. Then a few months later he had severe headaches. He went into the hospital for a checkup and was dead in two days. Brain cancer.

"A pastor friend of the family flew in to preach at the funeral. On the plane he sat down next to a youth. They began to talk; the pastor shared Charles's story, and the young boy gave his life to Jesus Christ before the plane landed. In New Orleans the pastor changed flights. On the next leg of his journey he sat next to a young woman. She, too, inquired where he was going, and he told her the story about Charles. Before the plane landed, she had accepted Jesus Christ as her Savior. The funeral was an occasion to praise the Lord for all He had done in Charles's life. After the funeral, two men accepted Christ on the sidewalk outside the chapel. Charles's body was flown to his hometown for burial. During the ceremony, I couldn't take my eyes off the face of the young widow. She was radiant with an inner peace and joy. During the past year she and Charles had come to know the joy in praising God for all things. She told me, 'Death is swallowed up in victory' (I Cor. 15:54). I have no reason to weep. Praise God!"

The two letters told of similar circumstances, but what a difference. One is a story of defeat, the other of victory. One sees from the human viewpoint, the other from the viewpoint of Christ.

The Bible tells us that we *can* have the viewpoint of Christ.

"Let this mind be in you, which was also in Christ Jesus" (Phil. 2:5

KJV). "And be constantly renewed in the spirit of your mind" (Eph. 4:23 *Amplified Bible*).

Paul wasn't suggesting an impossibility. The key words in his passages are "let" and "be renewed." We cannot give ourselves the viewpoint of Christ, but God will renew our minds if we *let* Him.

If we are willing to let it happen, we can tell God and expect Him to bring it about. Our part then is to *believe* it has happened.

David wanted to be in oneness with God's will for his life, yet he knew he couldn't change his own rebellious heart. He cried out to God: "*Remove* from me the way of falsehood and unfaithfulness [to You], and graciously *impart* Your law to me. I have *chosen* the way of truth and faithfulness; Your ordinances have I set before me... I will [not merely walk, but] run the way of Your commandments, when *You give me a heart that is willing*" (Psa. 119:29-30, 32 *Amplified Bible*).

David knew that the only action within his power was to choose to will the right way. God had to remove the wrong and impart the right and give David a willing heart.

God will do the same for us if we choose to let Him, then stand firm in faith, believing it is done. Whatever circumstances come into our lives, we are to praise and thank God for them, because they are His way of working out His perfect plan for us. The circumstances are His way of removing the wrong, imparting the right, and giving us a willing heart.

Praise releases the power of God into our lives and circumstances, because praise is faith in action. When we trust God fully, He is free to work, and He *always* brings victory. It may be a victory that changes circumstances, or a victory *in* the circumstances. Death may be turned away, or made to lose its sting.

Praise is a permanent acceptance of what God has brought into our lives. We enter this attitude of praise by an act of our will, by a decision to praise God regardless of how we feel.

"What time I am afraid, I will ... trust ... You," wrote David. "By [the help of] God I will praise His Word; on God I lean, rely and confidently put my trust" (Psa. 56:3-4 *Amplified Bible*).

"My heart is fixed, O God, my heart is fixed: I will sing and give praise" (Psa. 57:7 KJV).

6

Good-bye Grumblings

Have you ever stepped outside your door on a beautiful, clear, sunny day, taken a deep breath of fresh air, and thanked God for His wonderful creation?

But what if the next morning is gray and rainy? Does it automatically make you feel a little depressed as you look out the window? Maybe you don't say it out loud, but how do you feel?

Are you in the habit of thanking God only for what you want? And are you in the habit of grumbling just a little when things don't go the way you like?

So what's wrong with a little complaining? It's no big thing. What difference does it make?

It makes *all* the difference in the world. *Everything* depends on how we respond to the little things in life.

A marriage counselor will tell you that a marriage usually breaks up over little things. It takes only a small nail to puncture a tire. A small mistake by a mechanic can cause the crash of a giant airliner. A misunderstanding can start a war. One angry word leads to a shooting. Little things mean a lot, because this is the level where we live, down at the nitty-gritty of our attitude at the breakfast table, or in the long check-out line at the supermarket on a Friday afternoon.

Grumbling comes so easy to all of us that we often don't realize what we're doing. But grumbling is the very opposite of thanksgiving; a complaint is the opposite of trust; a murmur against your wife when she burns your toast is the opposite of loving acceptance.

The dictionary defines a complaint as an accusation. By complaining and grumbling you are actually accusing God of mismanaging the details of your day. The attitude of praise releases the power of God

80

into our lives, and the attitude of murmuring and complaining blocks that power.

"And don't murmur against God and his dealings with you, as some of them did, for that is why God sent His Angel [of death] to destroy them. All these things happened to them as examples—as object lessons to us—to warn us against doing the same things; they were written down so that we could read about them and learn from them . . . " (I Cor. 10:10-11).

Paul was speaking about the behavior of the Israelites on their wanderings from Egypt to the Promised Land. So what did they do and what were the terrible consequences?

"The people were . . . complaining about all their misfortunes, and the Lord heard them. His anger flared against them because of their complaints . . . " (Num. 11:1).

Moses had led the Israelites out of Egypt, and God had given them some remarkable signs of His presence and concern for them. He had parted the Red Sea, allowing them to walk across on dry land, and later brought the water back over the heads of the Egyptian soldiers pursuing them. God promised to lead His people to the Promised Land; He promised to feed them in the wilderness, and to drive their enemies out before them—if they would only trust Him. As a sign, God's presence went with them in the form of a pillar of dust in the daytime, and a pillar of fire at night.

But the Israelites didn't trust God. They complained bitterly, first because of a lack of food and water, and later because they didn't like the taste of the water God gave them. They grew tired of the diet God had provided for them. They fussed and complained about petty little things. And what were the consequences?

Patiently, God humored His murmuring children. Again and again He met their needs, until it became obvious that they would not learn. When they got tired of the taste of manna, and wanted meat instead, God said that He would give them meat, not just for one day or two days, but for a whole month, "until [you are satiated and vomit it up violently, and it] comes out at your nostrils, and is disgusting to you; because you have rejected and despised the Lord . . . " (Num. 11:20 *Amplified Bible*).

Forty years the Israelites wandered, and every time something went wrong, they complained bitterly and wanted to go back to the fleshpots of Egypt.

Why did it take them forty years to cover less than two hundred miles? Even with women and children and cattle, they could have covered the distance in a few weeks. They were delayed because they

81

murmured and refused to trust that God would keep His promise to take care of their every need.

When the Israelites first came to the border of their Promised Land, they discovered that giants already lived there, in fortified cities. Instead of rejoicing at the obstacles, praising God who had promised to drive all their enemies out before them, the Israelites turned against Moses and demanded to be taken back to the fleshpots of Egypt. They accused Moses of having tricked them and fooled them.

Only two men, Joshua and Caleb, who had seen the giants and the fortified cities, trusted that God would keep His promise and give the Israelites the land. But no one listened to Joshua and Caleb.

This was the last straw. God vowed to let the Israelites stew in their own complaints. Not one of the complainers would live to set foot on the Promised Land. Instead, the nation of Israel would wander in the wilderness for forty years, until a new generation would be grown up. *They* would be allowed to enter, led by Joshua and Caleb, the only two who would survive the wilderness years.

"God was patient with them forty years, though they tried his patience sorely; he kept right on doing his mighty miracles for them to see. 'But,' God says, 'I was very angry with them, for their hearts were always looking somewhere else instead of up to me, and they never found the paths I wanted them to follow' " (Heb. 3:10).

Petty complaining kept the Israelites out of their Promised Land.

Our complaints and murmurings against God in the little things can keep us from entering into the perfect plan He has for our lives.

"Beware then of your own hearts, dear brothers, lest you find that they, too, are evil and unbelieving and are leading you away from the living God" (Heb. 3:12).

The cause of the Israelites' murmuring was unbelief, and unbelief is at the root of every one of our little complaints.

Unbelief kept the Israelites out of Canaan. But God wanted to do more for them than just bring them into a geographical location. God's Promised Land was also to be a place of perfect rest, an attitude of perfect trust and peace of mind.

"Although God's promise still stands—his promise that all may enter his place of rest—we ought to tremble with fear because some of you may be on the verge of failing to get there after all . . . For only we who believe God can enter into his place of rest. He has said, 'I have sworn in my anger that those who don't believe me will never get in' " (Heb. 4:1,3).

God has a place of perfect rest prepared for us now. And I don't mean after death, I mean *now*. It is that state of perfect trust in Him that we can all enter into on faith. But in order to do so, we must give up our sin of unbelief, our grumblings, murmurings, and complaints. Unbelief is a serious offense against God.

"The world's sin is unbelief in me," said Jesus (John 16:9).

Unbelief, like all sin, is a deliberate act of rebellion against God. We can choose to believe or not to believe.

Webster defines unbelief as a "withholding of belief: incredulity or skepticism: a rejection of what is asserted."

If unbelief is a deliberate withholding of belief, then we are responsible for our action, and we must do something about it.

The first step in dealing with any sin is confession.

For years I had proudly told myself that I rarely grumbled, that is, I rarely grumbled out loud. I had cultivated and maintained a smiling facade, but I was a habitual grumbler inside. Of course, as long as I didn't think I was guilty of grumbling, I never improved.

I thought *my* kinds of complaints were legitimate. I grumbled when I didn't get enough sleep and had to get out of bed in the morning without feeling rested. I grumbled under my breath if the bathroom was messed up by another member of my family; and I grumbled over my hurried breakfast. I grumbled when things went wrong at the office, and when people didn't do what I expected of them. I grumbled over bills, and when my car wouldn't start, or when I hit a red light on my way to anywhere. I grumbled when I had to work late at the office and didn't get to bed on time; and the next morning I started all over again.

When finally the Holy Spirit began to show me what the Bible had to say about thanking God in everything, I began to realize that I'd been doing the opposite for years and never thought a thing about it.

The first step toward rehabilitation was to admit to myself that I was a habitual grumbler.

I believe that the most effective way to deal with our sins is to be specific about them. We admit them, confess them, ask God's forgiveness, and make a clear-cut decision not to fall into that sin again. We then ask God to remove the sin from us and to give us increased faith and strength to withstand any temptation. At last we thank Him for it and proceed on faith, knowing that it has been done.

Once we make an agreement with God not to grumble, and promise instead to thank Him for every little thing that used to make us grumble, we can expect Him to go to work.

We can't change ourselves from unbelieving grumblers to thankful, cheerful believers. God has to do the changing. We make the decision to quit grumbling and start thanking and praising God, but it is God's power that works the transformation. Our job is to keep our eyes on Jesus and thank God for what *He* is able to do.

In practice, we will find that God will bring into our lives the very kinds of circumstances that used to trigger our grumbling. When we see them coming, we can thank and praise God, because He's using those very incidents to bring about the change in us. Before, they made us stumble; now they will show us God's strength. They will serve to increase our faith.

Accepting every little thing that happens with joy and thanksgiving will release the power of God in and through us, and we will soon experience a *feeling* of joy as well. But don't look for the feeling as a sign. Our praise and thanksgiving must be based on faith in God's Word, not on our feelings.

One of the things I'd grumbled about for years was my lack of musical talent. Whenever I heard beautiful music, I failed to enjoy it fully, because it always made me wish I could play an instrument or sing beautiful solos.

Then one day I was listening to a concert, and the question came into my mind, "Are you thankful that you can't play a musical instrument?"

I recognized the source of the question as the Holy Spirit and squirmed in my seat.

"No, Lord, I guess I'm not."

"Are you willing to be?"

"Yes, Lord, I'm willing, and I understand that this will be your will for me. You could have arranged to give me a musical talent and have it trained if you wanted to, so I thank you for me, just as you wanted me to be."

As I said it, a great peace flowed into me, and I realized that I was actually happy to be as I am.

"What I wanted you to learn is this," the Holy Spirit said: "If you could make beautiful music, you would please some people, but when you give praise you always please God."

My lack of musical talent was never a shortcoming in God's eyes, only in my own. *I* was the one who was dissatisfied with the way God had made me. He was never dissatisfied.

There are people who spend their lives wishing they could have a special talent and an opportunity to develop it. They grumble and complain inside because they are sure that given the right breaks in life, they might have become a movie star, TV personality, baseball hero, business tycoon, or doctor.

Do you have a favorite grumble about your own life? Do you say to yourself that if you could only have a chance to live it over again, you'd be in a different profession, a different neighborhood, a different marriage?

Can you accept that God has you right now exactly where He wants you? That He hasn't overlooked a thing? That He wasn't helpless to interfere back when you made what you think of as your wrong choice?

Sure, there is such a thing as a wrong choice. We've been talking in this book about our responsibility to choose and the consequences of the right and wrong choices. But the promise of God is that He makes all things, including our own wrong choices, work out for good when we trust Him.

It is possible that you are in a job or in a situation God plans to move you out of. Still, it is essential that *right now* you accept your present situation with joy and thank God for it. As we thank God for every difficulty, submitting to His will at every turn, He is able to move us into the spot where He wants us.

Remember, He was able to move the heathen King Cyrus into the perfect spot at the right time even when Cyrus didn't know God. So you can be sure that if God had wanted you to be somewhere else at this very moment, He would have had you there. Your task right now is to thank Him for where you are at the *present*.

If God, by His Holy Spirit, shows you that you made a wrong choice fifteen years ago when you deliberately chose to go against what you then knew to be God's will for you, confess that wrong choice to Him now, ask His forgiveness, thank Him for it, and ask Him to guide you in making right anything you may have done to wrong others. Then turn the rest of your life, as of this moment, completely over into God's hands and trust that He now is in complete charge. *Now* praise and thank Him for your *present* circumstances exactly as they are in every detail.

You may discover God's power going to work to move you out of your present circumstances very quickly, or you may find that God's power is transforming you in the midst of the circumstances. Whatever happens, continue to thank Him. For He is in charge.

A Christian businessman made a deeper commitment of his life to Christ, and shortly thereafter found himself laid off from his highly-paid job as an executive. The man searched for another job, but cutbacks in the industry made positions scarce. His family suffered from the financial stress, and his anxieties increased as the bills mounted and his prayers seemed unanswered.

He had been unemployed for a year when he heard me speak one Saturday night about being thankful for all things. It suddenly dawned on him that God probably had a good reason for not having led him to a job, and he began to thank God for his unemployment and for every hardship he and his family were suffering as a result.

All day Sunday he continued to praise God, and he discovered that all his fears and resentments concerning the situation were decreasing. In their place, he felt genuine joy.

Early Monday morning the phone rang. Another executive wanted to know if he could go to work for him.

"Yes, I'm available," said the man.

"How soon can you start?"

"Tomorrow."

"Then be here at 9 a.m., ready to start."

His new job gave an excellent salary, but more important, he was in direct contact with groups of businessmen daily. His witness for Christ led one man after the other to accept the Lord as his Savior.

The businessman told me, "As long as I carried a spark of fear and resentment over my situation, I was blocking God from doing what He wanted to with my life. As soon as I was able to trust Him and praise Him for my life exactly as it was, He was able to take over and place me where He wanted me."

A young teacher was spending her summer vacation in the mountains when a letter was mailed from the superintendent's office telling her to report for a conference concerning next year's assignment. She didn't get the letter, and when she didn't show up for the conference, her job was given to someone else. When she returned from her vacation, she discovered that she was unemployed.

Her first impulse was to panic and go home to her parents in another state. School was to start in two weeks; there were no job openings in the district; and she had heavy financial obligations from her college days.

This young lady had just read *Prison to Praise* and recognized her present situation as an opportunity to practice what she'd learned. She deliberately quenched the impulse to panic, thanked God that He had allowed her to lose her job, and thanked Him for His perfect plan for her life.

For two days she praised God, fighting back every temptation to despair. On the third day a neighbor talked to her across the back fence.

"You know, you really ought to be teaching in a Christian school," she said. "Why don't you call the principal of the school where my son goes?"

The young teacher did, and discovered to her surprise that a position as first-grade teacher had been left suddenly vacant. She was interviewed and got the job.

"I know that God was able to take over the situation because I trusted Him enough to praise Him," she said. "If I'd pulled my usual old trick of panicking and running home to Mom and Dad, I might still have been unemployed and fussing at God for not looking after me."

Her new job suited her far better than the old one. She was able to freely share her faith in the classroom, and could openly pray with several of the children who had behavior problems.

God had a perfect plan and a perfect place for the young teacher and for the Christian businessman. He closed the doors to the jobs they had held and thought they wanted, and He opened the right doors when they trusted Him and praised Him *for* their unemployment.

Resentment and fear, grumbling and complaining, cause delays in the unfolding of God's plan for us. He has a perfect time plan, and we must realize that His timing doesn't always coincide with ours.

I had always been very punctual, and was proud of my ability to organize and make proper use of "the Lord's time." Then one day I found myself on a plane enroute to El Paso, Texas, where I was to speak at a convention of businessmen. I was glancing nervously at my watch. It was moving toward 2:30 p.m., and I had planned to be at the meeting at 2:00. *Now what possible good can come out of my being late for an engagement?* I wondered.

"Why are you letting this happen, Lord?" I asked, with just a trace of irritability. The only answer was another question:

"Are you thankful you are late?"

"That's not the point," I argued back. "Those poor people who arranged for me to come, and paid my expenses, are expecting me there on time. They are the ones who'll have to learn to be thankful."

Are you thankful? The thought persisted.

The truth suddenly dawned on me. I wasn't really moved by concern for the people at the meeting. *I* was the one who was upset. *I* wasn't trusting that God was handling the situation right. I was fussing and arguing over His management of "my" time.

"I'm sorry, Lord," I whispered. "I *do* believe you know best how to manage my time. If you're letting me be late, it must be part of your perfect plan, and I thank you for it. I turn the management of my time over to you and trust you to work it out for good."

I leaned back in my seat and drew a breath of relief. My watch said 2:45, but I felt perfect peace. At that moment the stewardess walked past, and her watch came into sharp focus before my eyes. It read 1:45.

I sat up. "Miss, your watch says 1:45. Are you sure that is correct?"

"Yes, sir, it is. We've just crossed into another time zone, and it is now 1:45."

I chuckled to myself. "Thank you, Lord, for teaching me how silly it is to worry about the time."

87

As the plane flew on, the time moved past 2:00, and I felt a twinge of anxiety again. At 2:15 we were coming in for landing at El Paso, but it looked like I would still be a few minutes late.

"Lord, I'm sorry I'm impatient," I muttered. "But I've never been late to a meeting before, and I don't understand why you're letting it happen now."

"Are you thankful?"

"All right, Lord," I said. "I *will* to be thankful. Thank you that it is now 2:20, and I'm exactly where I am."

When I walked off the plane, my watch said 2:25.

I pulled the convention schedule out of my pocket to check on the address, and my eyes fell on the time for the meeting. It said 2:30!

I ran to the nearest cabstand. *This is beautiful, Lord,* I thought. *You've been able to teach me a lesson about trusting your management of my time, without hurting anybody else.* (Incidentally, that is *always* the way God operates. We may think that others are hurt by our mistakes, but God is in complete control of their lives also, and He loves them as He loves us.)

The cabdriver looked at me expectantly. "Where to, Sir?"

"The El Paso Hilton Inn," I gasped. "I need to get there as quickly as possible!"

The cabdriver chuckled and pointed across the street.

"There it is, right in front of you!"

I walked through the door into the convention hall and glanced at my watch. It was exactly 2:30. The men were walking up to the speakers' table, and I filed up behind them to take my seat.

God's timetable is precise to the minute. How great it is to know that we're on His schedule.

Release the timekeeping of your life to Him. He will get you where He wants you, when He wants you there, if you trust Him. His schedule is good for every appointment and every hour of our lives. God doesn't force His time plan on us, but if we give our days and hours to Him, it is His business to get us where He wants us on His time.

That doesn't mean we can sit down in our soft seats and say, "If the Lord wants me there, He'll have to get me there. I'm just going to sit here and doze until He moves me."

We've got to do our part, but that is *not* to worry about the timekeeping. We do our best, get up on time in the morning, prepare in time for appointments, then thank Him for whatever happens—even if we oversleep, get delayed unexpectedly, or are interrupted by a talkative neighbor or demanding child.

God has a double purpose in teaching us to trust and praise Him in everything. It releases His power into *our* situation, and it also draws others to Him.

I once worked with a choir-leader who was a perfectionist. Every detail of the music for each service was planned and performed with precision, but the choir-leader always performed under a strain, and his tension was transmitted to the choir. They sang with excellence, but without joy.

One day the choir-leader dropped by for a chat in my office.

"Bob, I think you would be more relaxed and experience much joy in your music if you began to thank God for everything that happens," I said.

He looked at me in silence for some time, then said, "I've been watching you these past six months. At first I thought you were putting on a front. No one could be that joyful all the time." He smiled. "I made several mistakes with the choir, and you always reacted with joy. . . I don't understand how you do it, but I'd like to have the same attitude."

We talked until the time for choir-rehearsal, and Bob left my office in a hurry. He hadn't had time for any preparations, and I wondered how he would respond to the unexpected challenge.

Later he told me, "I was getting really tense thinking about all the music and equipment I hadn't prepared, but then it dawned on me: this was exactly the kind of situation we'd talked about thanking God for, so I thanked Him. Just then, four members of the choir came in the door. They were early for rehearsal and asked, 'What can we do to help you get ready?' Nothing like that had ever happened in the months I had led the choir.

"I was amazed. 'Thank you, God,' I prayed. 'You really took care of that problem quickly!' "

The rest of the day Bob had wandered in a half-daze. He had never realized before that God was personally concerned with the details of his life, and that God's power would be released as soon as he relaxed and was thankful in every circumstance. The discovery completely changed Bob's attitude to his music ministry.

The next time he sang a solo, he made several mistakes, something that ordinarily would have plunged him into despair. But instead of getting more tense with each wrong note, he offered up thanks to God Who allowed it to happen. As a result, he experienced increasing joy as the song progressed, and we who listened could see the happiness radiate from his face and hear the new dimension of joy in his singing.

Bob's relationship with the congregation also changed markedly. He had been greeting us with a glum "Hello"; now he beamed and said, "Good morning! Isn't it a beautiful day!"

Wearing a glum face may not seem like a sin, until we consider the fact that it expresses the very opposite of a happy, hopeful faith, and as such is actually an attitude of unbelief.

We all know the expression, "Well, we all have our bad days and our ups and downs." This is careless, dangerous thinking, because it suggests that bad days and ups and downs are a normal part of the Christian life. The Bible says that our *outward* circumstances may go up and down, be bad or good, but our *inner* attitude is to be a permanent state of rejoicing in Christ.

"I have learned how to get along happily whatever the circumstances may be," Paul wrote from a jail cell. "I know now how to live when things are difficult and I know how to live when things are prosperous. In general and in particular I have learned the secret of facing either plenty or poverty. I am ready for anything through the strength of the one who lives within me" (Phil. 4:11-13 *Living Bible* and Phillips).

The consequences of our failure to be thankful in the little things are not always apparent to us, but once I was taught a stern lesson.

It was a busy morning in our chaplain's office at Fort Benning, and everything seemed to go wrong. The senior man in charge had not showed up for work, and none of the others seemed to know what to do. Telephones were ringing, work was piling up, and I began to feel impatient with the man who had not reported for duty. Of course, my attitude didn't make him arrive, nor did it improve the situation. I grumbled under my breath through most of a miserable day.

The next day the man returned and explained that he had gone to the hospital where he was told that he had a cancerous growth in his sinus. Overcome at the news, he'd gone home to spend the day in bed, not caring if he ever got up again.

I was overwhelmed with remorse. I'd fussed over the insignificant delays at the office, instead of thanking God for the man who was absent. My grumblings had effectively put me out of commission as a channel for God's love and power flowing toward the sick man that day.

It is important that we learn to respond with trust and praise in all situations, whether or not the consequences are apparent to us. As we learn to push the praise button instead of the panic button, our lives and our attitudes are changed, whether the situation confronting us is a dramatic event or a minor irritation.

Once a man was driving home from work on icy roads. He misjudged the road conditions and slid through a stop sign and into another car. No one was injured, but the cars were badly damaged, and the responsible driver was angry with himself for having made a stupid mistake. Then he remembered having read recently about praising God for everything.

"Thank you for this accident, Lord," he prayed.

Immediately a silent voice whispered in his head, "Don't be stupid. You've made a bad mistake already. Are you going to make it w rse by pretending you're gla bout it?"

"But God has promised to make it work for good," he argued back.

"You'll never see anything good come out of *this*!"

"If I thank God, I will," the man persisted.

He continued to be thankful for the accident, yet nothing outwardly dramatic happened as a result. The other driver wasn't led to Christ, and no one seemed to react to his joyful attitude at the garage.

So what difference did it make how he reacted?

As the day progressed, something very remarkable was happening *in* that man. The more he thanked God, the more a new kind of peace spread inside him. Toward noon he discovered that something like bubbling laughter kept welling up from within, and each time he repeated his thanks to God for the car accident, he could feel something being released, like the untying of tight knots, deep within him.

He had been an average Christian, but from that day on his life was never again the same. He had entered a new dimension of victorious living in Christ—all because of his determination to recognize God's hand in something he had first thought was his own stupid mistake and a stroke of bad luck.

Another man heard me speak about praising God for everything and promised God from that moment he would be thankful for everything that happened to him.

He and his family drove home from the meeting through a snowstorm in below-zero weather. They arrived home late at night, and the moment they stepped in the front door, they knew something was wrong. The house was ice-cold, and the furnace was dead.

The family huddled upstairs while the man walked down to the basement to check the furnace. He knew nothing about furnaces and had no idea what might be wrong

He stood staring at the cold, silent furnace, and his first impulse was to pray that God would help him get it going again. Without heat in the house, he would have to take his family to a warm shelter for the night.

Then the thought came to him, "Are you thankful now?"

He had to admit that he'd been too upset over his cold house and freezing family to be thankful.

"I'm sorry, Lord, I forgot," he prayed. "But I know you must have planned this for our good, so thank you, God, for this furnace, just as it is."

At that moment a very distinct suggestion came into his mind: "Check the fan!"

The fan? I don't even know where it is!

"Look behind the plate on the right side," came the thought.

He found a screwdriver and began removing the plate. The whole scene suddenly struck him as ridiculous. Was he just imagining things? Was the fan really behind that plate? But if God was really at work giving him this direct kind of help, he couldn't stop now, he reasoned.

His fingers were numb with cold, but the plate came off—and there was the fan.

Now what? he thought.

"Look for the fan belt; it is off."

It was too dark to see inside the furnace, so he got a flashlight and directed the beam down the small opening in the furnace. There was the fan belt, lying loose. He slipped it over the drive shaft on the fan and removed his arm from the narrow opening. The furnace remained cold and silent.

"What now?" he prayed.

"Turn the furnace switch," came the suggestion.

As soon as he turned the switch, the furnace came alive with happy dancing flames, and the man ran upstairs to share with his family how God had blessed them with a cold furnace.

Had the man *not* responded to the crisis by praising God and expecting Him to work it all for good, he and his family would have suffered inconvenience and hardship. The cold furnace was a God-given opportunity to learn in practice that praise releases the power and guidance of God.

Following the furnace incident, that man's life was changed. He began to listen for the voice of God in all situations, and today has developed a rare sensitivity to the promptings of the Holy Spirit. His open ear to the guidance of God has made him a channel for God's power in the lives of others also.

The first step was an act of faith, believing that a cold furnace on a dark, snowy night was an expression of God's loving concern for his and his family's welfare. He could have passed up that first opportunity, and I am sure that God would have provided other challenges. You and I are confronted with opportunities to recognize God's hand in every situation of our daily lives. How many opportunities do we pass up?

The results of our reactions are cumulative. With each positive step of faith, it becomes easier to believe. In the same way, each time we allow unbelief to deny God's presence and love in a difficult situation, the negative results heap up, and it becomes increasingly difficult to muster our will to exercise any faith at all. The more we grumble, the more we become entangled in the web of defeat. Many little grumbles add up to overwhelming mountains of depression.

A Christian nurse wrote of years she had spent in misery.

"It seemed like little things always upset me and caused irritation. Gradually my life was getting more and more miserable. I prayed for God to help me, but nothing happened. I started taking pills to get going in the morning and pills to go to sleep at night. Every day began with the agony of having to get out of bed. I couldn't cope with my own housework. At the hospital I was breaking under the strain of caring for the patients.

"Every day was worse than the one before. I couldn't even do little things I had been able to do with ease a few months before. I was sinking into such a depression that I prayed for God to let me die. Living was sheer hell."

Then one day she read *Prison to Praise.*

"It was like a light of hope had been turned on inside me," she wrote. She determined to praise God for everything, and made a long list of things to be thankful for, beginning with the circumstances that had caused her so much strain. The results soon began to show up.

"All I can think of now is, *What a wonderful change in my life there has been—since Jesus came into my heart!* I no longer have a horrible fear of failure hanging over me. Things don't irritate and upset me. When something appears to go wrong, I just look up and say, 'Thank you, Lord!' and it really puts a song in my heart!"

Whether you are surrounded by what seem to you like mountains of accumulated misery, or just irritating little molehills, the turning point is the same. Confess your complaining and murmuring as sin, and promise God that you'll be thankful from now on.

You make the decision and determine to stand on it in faith; God will furnish the strength to do it. Once you've made your commitment, the opportunities to thank God may come in little or big packages, but they'll come.

At a retreat near Fort Benning, several young people made a promise to thank God for all things. The next day one of the soldiers was notified that a favorite uncle had been killed in a tractor accident on the farm. Immediately the thought came to the soldier, "Now see what happened! You made that silly commitment to praise God. Your uncle wasn't even a Christian!"

The soldier recognized the source of that thought, and resisted the temptation to complain to God about his uncle's death. Instead he prayed, "God, you know how much I loved my uncle, but you loved him more, so you must have had a good reason for letting him die. I'll just thank you and praise you for doing what was best."

The soldier felt a peace about his uncle's death, but was unable to shake off a concern for his cousin who had just recently accepted Christ as his Savior. How would he take his father's death? The soldier wanted to go home for the funeral in order to encourage his cousin, but he was unable to get leave.

"Okay, God," he prayed. "You know all about my cousin, so I'll just thank you that I can't go." He thought he would call home and ask his parents to convey a message to his cousin, and stepped into a phone booth to make the call.

When a voice answered at the other end, he immediately recognized his cousin. "How are you?" he blurted out in surprise.

"I'm praising the Lord," came the answer. "We're all so glad that Dad accepted Christ several days before the accident. He had time to tell everybody what God had done for him, and we know it was God's will that he go to heaven now."

The soldier returned to the retreat to share with the others what had happened. A chaplain's wife who was there promised God she would thank Him for everything in her life.

Driving home that evening, she had her first opportunity. In eighteen years of driving, she'd never had a traffic ticket. This time she was asked to pull over to the side of the road and an MP who'd been following her at a distance gave her a ticket for going through an intersection without making the required stop.

She explained to the MP that he had made a mistake. Another car looking just like hers had failed to stop at the intersection, speeding past her as she came to a careful halt. The policeman did not accept her story, and her first impulse was to be angry and complain about the injustice. Then she remembered her promise to be thankful in everything.

"God, I trust this is your will," she prayed. "I will praise you for the whole experience." Suddenly she discovered that her inner being was flooded with joy.

The next day she returned to the retreat and told us what had happened.

"Isn't it marvelous?" she said. "We don't have to worry about being treated unfairly or taken advantage of. Even *those* circumstances become a source of joy and strength when we see God's hand in them and give thanks."

Others are drawn to Christ when we praise God. If we grumble and complain as bitterly as our non-Christian friends over the many little upsetting incidents of our days, others conclude that our faith does no

94

more for us than having no faith does for them. Unless they can see, in the nitty-gritty of our daily lives, that Christ makes a difference, how can we expect them to believe when we say they need Jesus?

It isn't what we say, but what we are and what we do that draws others to the Christ-life in us. Nowhere is this more apparent than in our daily lives. How do we react to delays and difficulties on the job, in emergencies, in everyday encounters? Do we react in such a way that no one sees anything different about us? Or does our reaction cause them to stop and say, "Something is different about that person. He's got something I need"?

One couple read *Prison to Praise* and were convinced that God wanted them to be thankful for everything. One night they were awakened at 2:30 a.m. by the sound of breaking glass. The man looked outside and saw that all the windows in his car had been smashed by a group of kids who were fast disappearing around the corner.

The couple agreed that God had given them an opportunity to praise Him, and they knelt by their bed, giving thanks for what had happened.

The next morning the man took his car to a garage and explained what had happened.

"Thank God," he said. "I'm sure He has a wonderful purpose behind it all."

The owner of the garage shook his head.

"If something like that happened to me, I'd see to it that those young punks were made to pay," he said.

The customer smiled. "That isn't necessary," he explained. "God is in charge of the situation; I don't need to be upset about it."

The garage-owner stared at him for a moment, then said, "I've been a Christian for years, but I never heard about praising God for vandalism."

They talked on, and the customer told the garage-owner about the baptism in the Holy Spirit and the power of God released through praise.

"Hold it," said the garage-owner. "I've heard about the baptism in the Holy Spirit till I've gotten sick of it. I have one customer who talks about nothing else. But tell me more about praising God. That sounds interesting."

The customer explained that he thought the two subjects were one, since both had to do with complete trust and commitment to God. Finally the garage-owner accepted an invitation to attend a meeting of Spirit-filled businessmen, and at the meeting he experienced the baptism in the Holy Spirit for himself.

Next he committed himself to praising God for everything, and the first item on his list was his business. It had been sliding toward bankruptcy for two years.

The next afternoon one of his employees came with bad news; he had been in an accident, wrecking their truck. This could be the last straw, toppling the business.

The garage-owner looked at his young employee, who stood pale and trembling, obviously expecting an outburst of temper from his boss. Instead the garage-owner smiled, put his arm around the young man's shoulders and said, "Let us praise God for this accident and believe He will work it out for good!"

A routine insurance claim was submitted, and to the garage-owner's amazement, the settlement enabled him to pay urgent bills. The accident marked the turning point in his business, and his profits began to show a marked increase. It marked an even more important turning point in the life of the garage-owner who now experienced increasing joy and peace in every area of his life. In turn, a steady stream of customers came to know Jesus Christ as their Savior because they were impressed with his obvious joy.

When the joy of Christ is released in our lives, others are drawn to Him.

Once, after a late meeting, I walked into a restaurant and asked for a glass of milk. The waitress smiled and went to the kitchen to get my order. A moment later she reappeared with an angry frown on her face.

"I'm very sorry, sir, but someone has locked the refrigerator, and I can't get any milk for you."

"Thank the Lord!" I responded automatically.   The waitress looked puzzled.

"Why did you say that?"

"I have learned to be thankful for everything, because I believe that God works everything for good if you let Him."

"What religion are you?" she asked incredulously.

"Methodist."

"Well, I'm a Baptist, but I have never heard of being thankful for things like that!"

"Are you a Christian Baptist?" I asked.

"Well," she hesitated, "I think I am, but I've never been sure."

"You can be absolutely sure," I said. "Jesus came into the world to give us eternal life as a free gift. All we have to do is ask Him to forgive our sins and then believe that He does. I'd like to pray with you and ask God to give you this free gift if you want it."

The waitress nodded eagerly. "Yes, sir, I would like that!"

I touched her shoulder with my hand, we bowed our heads, and there in the empty restaurant, a few minutes after midnight, I prayed that

God would release her faith and give her assurance of eternal life through Christ.

Tears were running down her face.

"I've never felt like this before in my life," she said. "I feel as if a great burden has rolled off my back. I really do believe I'm a Christian now."

It may seem inconsequential to make a point out of being grateful for not getting a glass of milk when you want it, but as you learn to thank God for every little thing, God will use your praise to draw unhappy, weary people to Him. And He can turn their burden of worries and anxieties into pure joy and peace.

I was sitting in an Atlanta airport, waiting to board a plane, when a stranger suddenly picked up the briefcase I had placed on a low table beside me. I had left the latch open, and the contents spilled all over the floor. Papers flew in all directions, and I noticed my toothbrush, thrown out of its case, lying on the dirty floor. I stifled the impulse to be upset with the clumsy stranger and muttered under my breath, "Yes, Lord, I do thank you for this and I know you have some good reason for letting it happen."

The embarrassed stranger apologized and hastily began to pick up my scattered belongings. When I joined him, he looked up and said, "You don't remember me, do you?"

"No, I'm afraid I don't."

He explained that we had met briefly several months ago and that he had just now been walking through the terminal feeling tired and discouraged, asking God to lead him to someone who could help.

"I saw you and picked up your briefcase in order to sit down on the table next to you," he explained. "Now I know God led me to you. Will you please explain how you could remain completely undisturbed when I spilled your things all over the floor?"

I was more than happy to tell him how glorious it is to trust that all things work for good if we love God, and that little experiences like an upset briefcase are opportunities to thank God and watch Him work.

The man was amazed and asked several questions. When the time came for my plane to leave, he said, "Would you consider coming to Fort Lauderdale, Florida, as my guest, at your earliest convenience?"

It was my turn to be amazed. I had been praying that God would provide a way for me to go to Fort Lauderdale. I had heard much about what God had been doing in the lives of Christians there.

Paul wrote to the Christians at Philippi:

"In everything you do, stay away from complaining and arguing, so that no one can speak a word of blame against you. You are to live clean, innocent lives as children of God in a dark world full of people who are crooked and stubborn. Shine out among them like beacon lights, holding out to them the Word of Life. . . Whatever happens, dear friends, be glad in the Lord. I never get tired of telling you this and it is good for you to hear it again and again" (Phil. 2:14-16; 3:1).

It is our lack of complaining and our happiness in Christ that enables us to shine like beacons, holding out the Word of Life in a dark world. It was true in Philippi, and it is true today.

Let's quit our grumblings and praise the Lord for every dark and crooked thing we see around us. Do it, and watch God's light penetrate the darkness!

The Joy of the Lord

"The joy of the Lord is your strength," said the prophet Nehemiah (Neh. 8:10).

No wonder Jesus was so concerned that His disciples would understand that He had come, not only to purchase their salvation through His sacrifice on the cross, but also to provide them with the sustaining power of His joy.

"You haven't tried this before," He told them, "[but begin now]. Ask, using my name, and you will receive, and your cup of joy will overflow" (John 16:24).

The joy of the Lord is ours for the asking!

Jesus prayed for us before He was captured: "That *My joy* may be made full and complete and perfect in them—that they may experience *My delight* fulfilled in them, that *My enjoyment* may be perfected in their own souls, that they may have *My gladness* within them filling their hearts" (John 17:13 *Amplified Bible*).

Every born-again Christian knows that his salvation is a free gift. He was born again of the Holy Spirit when he accepted Jesus Christ as h Savior, *on faith*. Many Christians have come to discover that there is more to God's free gift than just being born again as a child of God. The baptism in the Holy Spirit can be claimed *on faith*. But very few of us seem to have realized that Jesus has already provided us with His joy. It is there to be claimed *on faith* with the rest of the package.

If the joy of the Lord is our strength, then it is obviously not something that comes last in a long line of attainments, sort of like the whipped topping on the cake. It is something we need from the start, something to sustain us and strengthen us in our task of carrying the Good News around the world.

Paul wrote to the Corinthians, "When I come, although I can't do much to help your faith, for it is strong already, I want to be able to do something about your joy: I want to make you happy, not sad" (II Cor. 1:24).

Paul didn't mean that he would *make* them happy by bringing nice gifts or provide pleasant circumstances. He intended to remind them of the joy they had already been given. He wanted them to practice rejoicing to cultivate the joy planted in them by the Holy Spirit.

Paul knew that the outward circumstances for an active Christian witness would always be filled with trials and suffering. His source of joy was his inward abiding in Christ.

"The Holy Spirit clearly ... affirms to me in city after city that imprisonment and suffering await me. But none of these things move me; neither do I esteem my life dear to myself, *if only I may finish my course with joy,* and the ministry which I have obtained of ... the Lord Jesus, faithfully to attest the good news ... of God's grace ... " (Acts 20:23-24 *Amplified Bible*).

If joy has already been given us by Jesus, why do most Christians live such joyless lives?

Jesus prayed that His joy would be perfected in us. What He means is that we can't make ourselves joyful anymore than we can save ourselves, give ourselves peace, or make ourselves more loving. What we *can* do is to choose to accept and trust what Jesus has done for us and allow Him to perfect His joy in us.

In practice, this means that we deliberately set out to practice joy, regardless of how we feel, trusting that God then goes to work, transforming our sorrows into pure joy, just as He has promised.

Love, joy, and peace are all part of the fruit of the Holy Spirit in us. Jesus told his disciples how they were to cultivate this fruit.

"I have loved you even as the Father has loved Me. Live within my love. When you obey me you are living in my love, just as I obey My Father and live in his love. *I have told you this so that you will be filled with my joy"* (John 15:9-11).

The source of joy was not to be found in happy circumstances, but in knowing Jesus' commandments, obeying them, and abiding in Him.

Jeremiah wrote, "Your words were found, and I ate them, and Your word was to me a joy and the rejoicing of my heart" (Jer. 15:16 *Amplified Bible*).

Joy is certainly something we are meant to feel. It is to be a happy, overflowing, pleasant experience. But joy does not depend on feeling.

We are not to rejoice because we feel joyful, rather we can expect to eventually feel joyful as a result of our rejoicing.

David had learned the secret of rejoicing. "Rejoice with trembling," he wrote in Psa. 2:11. "And now shall my head be lifted up above my enemies round about me; in His tent will I offer *sacrifices and shouting of joy;* I will sing, yes, I will sing praises to the Lord" (Psa. 27:6 *Amplified Bible*).

For a long time I thought that joy was something I would experience when I was satisfied and things were happy around me. Now I realize that joy doesn't spring up in my emotions, but is triggered by my will and is part and parcel of the life of praise.

"Let all the joys of the godly well up in praise to the Lord, for it is right to praise him," wrote David in Psa. 33:1.

Joy, thanksgiving, and praise belong together, and our commitment to praise and thank God for everything does not become complete until we've committed ourselves to rejoice in everything as well.

An elderly woman who had been filled with the Holy Spirit and had been an active Christian worker for years became crippled with arthritis. Years of pain had robbed her of any joy in living; the smallest household chore was an agony, and she experienced increasing depression.

She believed that God could heal, and had gone to healing meetings, but her condition only grew worse. One day she heard about the power in praising God for everything, and made up her mind to try it. Her task wasn't easy, since now every moment of her days and nights was filled with pain. But she was willing to be genuinely thankful for every part of her life, including her pain.

One day she moved slowly across her kitchen floor, carrying a tray of utensils. Suddenly the tray dropped, scattering items over the entire floor. Her painful back and stiff fingers made it impossible for her to bend over to pick anything up from the floor. Her usual reaction to dropping an object was to break down in tears of self-pity. But this time she remembered her promise to praise God.

"Thank you, Lord," she prayed, "for letting me drop everything on the floor. I believe you're working it to my good."

In a flash she became aware of other beings in the kitchen besides herself. She had been alone—yet now she sensed others present. Startled, she realized she was surrounded by angels. The angels were laughing and rejoicing, and she knew their joy was for her. Suddenly she understood.

Jesus told His disciples, "There is rejoicing among the angels of God over one sinner whose heart is changed" (Luke 15:10 Phillips).

She was certainly a saved sinner whose heart had been miraculously changed. For years she had been filled with self-pity and complaint against God for letting her suffer. She had begged Him to heal her, and inwardly had felt that God had let her down. At last she had seen that her grumbling was rooted in unbelief, and there was rejoicing among the angels when she trusted God enough to praise Him for the mishap with the tray of utensils.

She stood in the middle of her kitchen floor and felt herself saturated by the joy that filled the room. With a heart rejoicing she could thank God sincerely for allowing the suffering that had brought her such joy.

A short time later she attended a service where they offered prayer for the sick. Confidently, she walked forward. Always before, the painful awareness of her disease had crippled her ability to believe. Now her faith was not anchored in her feelings. She was free to believe, no matter how intense her pain was. That night she was instantly healed. All pain left, and the twisted joints became straight and whole.

We are such creatures of habit. For so long we've let our senses dictate our reactions. But Christ came to live in us so that His joy can become full and complete in us.

The initiative to rejoice can't come to us from our emotions, mind, or senses, but from the part of us that is spirit, born of the Holy Spirit. That's where our will resides, and the more we allow our will to take the initiative for our action, rather than giving in to our senses, the more we'll discover that we become increasingly able to respond to any situation with praise, joy and thanksgiving. Our old dependency on feeling will grow weaker, and as we persist, we'll discover that the joy originating in our will and spirit will spread to our senses as well.

What is begun as an act of obedience to God's Word, will eventually bring about in us a state of being where we sense, feel, think, and experience a real, overflowing praise, thanksgiving, and joy beyond anything we've ever known.

When we fully submit to God's will, so that all obstacles in us can be flushed away, and we can be molded, transformed, and renewed into perfect vessels for Him, then we'll also find that the joy of the Lord *is* complete in us.

For nearly twenty years I suffered with stomach trouble. Many foods gave me extreme discomfort. I'd gone the rounds of doctors and taken all kinds of medicines, but nothing helped.

I prayed and tried to believe that God would heal me, with no apparent result. Others prayed for me—Christian leaders well known for their effective ministry in healing, prayer groups, and friends—but the problem continued.

I claimed the promise Jesus gave in Mark 16 that not even poison could hurt me, and frequently ate whatever foods were served to me. But "apparent disaster" struck again and again, and I would be miserably ill, unable to sleep, and feel extremely sorry for myself.

I finally decided to accept on faith the fact that I had been healed by Christ's death for me, and to believe that the symptoms would go away when He was ready. For several years I rested on that assurance and thanked God for working in my life in this way for whatever good He wanted to accomplish.

Before I retired from the army, the doctors decided to operate on my stomach. They found nothing obvious to explain the years of pain I had gone through, and consequently could do nothing to improve my condition.

As I lay in my hospital bed after the operation, the pain increased in severity beyond anything I had endured before. Pain-killers or drugs had no effect. Hour after hour I lay without sleeping, feeling as if the darkness of the room was actually closing in on me. I thought I could almost reach out and touch the dark power of evil hovering around me, and I fought against the temptation to give in to the terror I felt. I didn't want to die but dreaded living in such misery.

At the moment when the blackness seemed darker than ever, I cried out, "Lord, I don't care what happens or how miserable I am, I thank you for this entire experience. I know you are going to bring something good out of it."

Instantly the darkness of the hospital room was shattered by a brilliant, white light, brighter than the sun. It was as bright as the light I'd seen in a vision several years before. At that time, the Holy Spirit had explained the vision to me. There was a dark cloud hovering over a sunny meadow, and above the cloud was a bright, white light. Up above the cloud was the state of joy and blessing Christ had already secured for us, but to get there, we had to climb on a ladder straight through the dark cloud of confusion and pain. Inside the cloud it was impossible to know what direction to take through the use of our ordinary sense-perception—sight, hearing, or feeling. The ladder could only be climbed on faith, and by praising God each step of the way. Climbing through that dark cloud, we would be stripped of our dependency on our senses and learn to trust God's Word. The ladder of praise would lift us right up into the heavenlies, to take our place there with Christ Jesus.

As I lay on my bed in the hospital room, my entire body flooded by that wonderful, brilliant light, I suddenly realized that what had once been a vision, now was a reality.

The years I had walked by faith, believing that God was using my

103

pain for good, were years of climbing through the cloud of darkness and uncertainty. Without the cloud, I would never have learned to let go of my reliance on my senses and feelings. Now I could wholeheartedly thank God for every circumstance of my life that added to the dark cloud. How else could I have learned to utterly trust in Him? How else could I have come to experience this beautiful saturation of light and joy?

When I returned home from the hospital, I discovered that God had done something about the condition of my stomach as well.

The foods that had once sent me into hours of pain no longer bothered me. I rejoiced in my new freedom to eat strawberries, apples, bananas, ice cream—all the things I had tried to stay away from for years.

Over the years, others had been healed instantly as I prayed for them, but God had chosen to strengthen my faith by letting me trust in His Word.

Praise does release the power of God to heal, but the healing is of secondary importance. As long as we're primarily concerned with our own comfort, our desire to be healed and free from physical pain, we've got the wrong perspective. Our concern actually amounts to a questioning of God's plan for us.

For years I'd been afraid of one day losing my teeth. Then one day my dentist told me that my gums were badly infected, and the bones around my teeth were deteriorating. X-rays showed the sad picture; I would soon lose my teeth!

Downhearted, I left the dentist's office. Of course I knew that I ought to be thanking God for my condition, but I wasn't very happy about it.

"Thank you, Lord," I said. "I'm grateful that you've allowed my teeth to get into such bad shape. I'm sure you know better than I do what's best for me, so I praise you, Lord."

Even as I prayed I began to feel more thankful, and when a friend came along, I told her about my new occasion to praise the Lord.

"Have you prayed for healing?" she asked.

"No," I said. "I've just now realized that losing my teeth isn't anything to fuss over, since it can't happen unless God allows it."

"I think God wants you to have perfect teeth," my friend said, placing her hand lightly on my shoulder. "Dear God," she prayed. "Thank you for letting Merlin's teeth get in such a rotten shape. We praise you and ask that you be glorified in this, so touch Merlin now and heal him completely."

Three days later I was back in the dentist's office and watched while he studied my new X-rays carefully. He had a concerned, puzzled look on his face, and once put the X-rays down to take another look in my mouth. He shook his head and muttered under his breath, and I thought, *Maybe they're worse than he expected.*

Finally the dentist stepped back, looked me over from head to foot, and asked, "What in the world have you done to your teeth?"

"Not a thing!"

"Then I don't understand." He looked from my old X-rays to the new ones. "Your bones are perfect, your gums are no longer infected and swollen—in fact your whole mouth looks perfect!"

I chuckled. How wonderful to know that God had healed me—but even better, healing was no longer the real issue. That little gnawing fear I'd carried with me about having false teeth was gone. I knew that with or without perfect teeth of my own, it was perfect union with Christ and trust in God's loving concern for every detail of my life that really mattered.

Recently I had a letter from a dear lady in New Hampshire. She lives alone with her teen-age son, and when she wrote me, she had been flat on her back and in constant pain after two major operations. She wrote:

"Praise God for His great faithfulness! I was very discouraged after my last operation, but someone gave me *Prison to Praise.* I decided to praise God for my illness and keep looking to Jesus. Since then my pain has not gone away, but I have come to know my Savior in a deeper way, and the Holy Spirit has ministered to me so wonderfully.

"Some of my friends have told me that God made me suffer in order to punish me. But I know this isn't so. Jesus has never accused me; instead He has taught me much about His love. These past months He has used His Word to show me things in my heart and life that shouldn't be there, feelings and thoughts unlike Christ. God in His wonderful love has forgiven me and healed every scar of old hurts in my life.

"I've learned to thank Jesus for the hard places, and even for the pain. I love Jesus with all my heart. I don't understand why He leads the way He does, but if I can be happy and 'take pleasure' in my infirmity (II Cor. 12:10), and in going this way for God, I certainly praise Him for it.

"I have to go back to the hospital for a possible third operation. I thank God for it, knowing that He will work in it for good. I know He can heal me, and I thank Him for whatever He decides in His love is best for me."

Her letter overflowed with genuine joy and gratitude. Her physical body was still in pain, but she had experienced a healing of her emotions and inner being and had entered into a wonderful relationship with God in Christ. Everything else, even her healing, had become secondary.

Oneness with God in Christ was the goal Paul was pressing toward. Jesus knew that His purpose for coming to earth was to remove the sin ba   · between man and God, so that once mor ·   Creator could be united with His creation, just as He had originally intended.

Before His crucifixion Jesus prayed for us:

"I am not praying for these alone, but also for the future believers who will come to me because of the testimony of these. My prayer for all of them is that they will be of one heart and mind, just as you and I are, Father—that just as you are in me and I am in you, so they will be in us, and the world will believe you sent me. I have given them the glory you gave me—the glorious unity of being one, as we are—I in them and you in me, all being perfected into one—so that the world will know you sent me and will understand that you love them as much as you love me. Father, I want them with me—these you've given me—so that they can see my glory. You gave me the glory because you loved me before the world began! O righteous Father [Father of goodness and truth], the world doesn't know you, but I do; and these disciples know you sent me. And I have revealed you to them, and will keep on revealing you so that the mighty love you have for me may be in them and I in them" (John 17:20-26).

Jesus prayed, and we know for certain that His prayer was answered. Paul assures us that we *have* been seated with Christ. Christ dwells in us. We are one in Him with the Father.

When we begin to grasp the full significance of these accomplished facts, everything else in our lives begin to take on the right perspective. The outer circumstances that once loomed out of proportion to our relationship with Christ and captured most of our attention can now be seen fitting perfectly into the plan that God is working in our lives. We still don't see the plan, but we *do* see Jesus Christ as Lord and Master, and we *know* that God has a plan and it is g   1

Many letters have come to me from people in prisons and peniten tiaries across the country since *Prison to Praise* was published.

One fellow wrote from death row:

"I've been sentenced to die in the electric chair. I know I have to die, and for a long time I had no hope for anything beyond death. Fear controlled all my thoughts, and I felt forsaken by God and man. Then I read *Prison to Praise*. It was as if my mind had become alive again. I dared believe that God is for real and is working in every life to draw us to accept His Son as Savior and Lord.

"I looked back on my own sordid life and realized that everything had happened with God's permission so that I might come to the point of reaching out for Him. I did reach out, and in one blinding instant I knew that God does work in all things for our good and His glory. For the first time I knew that my entire life was being blessed by God, and that by faith in His Son I belonged to Him. Now I am truly free and filled with His peace and joy."

Another prisoner wrote:

"I had learned to hate everyone and everything. No matter how hard I tried, I couldn't see any reason to be glad I was alive. Someone gave me *Prison to Praise,* and when I first read it I thought it was a bunch of nonsense. But the more I thought about it, the more I was tempted to try thanking God for my messy life. After all, I was at the bottom; what did I have to lose?"

"I began to go over the events of my life, one by one, as they came back to my memory. I thanked God that each incident was a part of His plan for me. The whole program seemed pretty foolish, but I forced myself to keep going. As I stuck with it, something began to happen inside of me. I began to think of God being personally involved in my mixed-up life. Could it really be true that He was interested in *me*? Events I'd forgotten pounded their way back into my mind. I'd thought of them as tragic before; now I began to see them as part of God's faithful drawing to convince me that I needed Him.

"I praised Him for every detail of my life; I thanked Him for the people who had hated me, mistreated me, lied about me, and betrayed me. I thanked Him for the ones I had hated, mistreated, lied about, and betrayed.

"A glowing peace began to flood me. God was healing all the bitter memories. The prison walls melted, and peace surrounded me instead. The walls and the bars can't make me a prisoner anymore. I'm free in Christ, praise God!"

Another letter came from a Christian in a top-security penitentiary in the West:

"Praise God! Attendance at our church and evening Bible-study groups is swelling. Last week three men accepted Christ as their Savior. Imagine what it would mean if three souls came to Jesus every week inside these walls! [A later letter told that in the next month twelve men accepted Christ and four received the baptism in the Holy Spirit.] We really appreciate the prayers of the brothers at Fort Benning. The Lord is making His presence felt in this institution like never before . . . God is answering our prayers and we will someday see many souls belong to Jesus among the prisoners here. What a blessing it has been to read *Prison to Praise*. We rejoice over the possibility of a tape-ministry inside the prison walls so that we can actually hear some of the teachings of our Christian brothers on the 'outside.'

"God is so great! Eight years ago I walked through these prison gates with a fresh ten-to-eighty year sentence for armed robbery. I thought my future held nothing but a policeman's bullet or oblivion through alcoholism. I had tried all the rehabilitation programs, but when I went out on parole I was drunk for a solid three months and twenty-five days until I was put back in prison. I'd honestly tried to change myself, but it was no use.

"Then six months ago, in an instant, Jesus Christ did the changing for me. I was transformed, just like it says in the Bible. 'Therefore, if any man is in Christ, he is a new creation; the old has passed away, behold, the new has come' (II Cor. 5:17 RSV). Since then, Jesus Christ has been working to clean up my life, letting His light shine over all the murky, cobwebby corners. Praise God! Nobody has a rehabilitation program worthy of mention, compared to the one Christ has to offer. Man cannot change the inner man, only Christ can!

"Praise the wonderful Jesus. He poured over me the light of God's love. The joy of living with Jesus becomes deeper day by day.

"Thank you for joining us in prayer for a continuing awakening among the prisoners, and for a strengthening of the new converts . . . Love from the brethren in Jesus."

That Christian brother is living and praising God in circumstances most of us would call dark and difficult. Yet for him, the perspective has become totally changed. He knows the joy of abiding in Jesus Christ, and everything else in his life has become secondary. He has learned to "rejoice evermore. Pray without ceasing. In every thing give thanks: for this is the will of God in Christ Jesus concerning you" (I Thess. 5:16-18 KJV).

John Wesley wrote in his comments on that passage, "*Rejoice evermore*—in uninterrupted happiness in God. *Pray without ceasing*—which is the fruit of always rejoicing in the Lord. *In everything give thanks*—which is the fruit of both of the former. This is Christian perfection. Farther than this we cannot go; we need not stop short of it. Our Lord has purchased joy as well as righteousness for us. It is the very design of the gospel, that being saved from guilt, we should be happy in the love of Christ. Thanksgiving is inseparable from true prayer: it is almost essentially connected with it. He that always prays is ever giving praise, whether in ease or pain, both for prosperity and for the greatest adversity. He blesses God for all things, looks on them as coming from Him, and receives them only for His sake; not choosing nor refusing, liking nor disliking anything, but only as it is agreeable or disagreeable to His perfect will" (*Notes on the New Testament*).

To live a life in uninterrupted happiness in God, looking on every circumstance as coming from God, and thanking Him for it—that is Christian perfection.

There is nothing haphazard about God's plan for our lives. Nothing, absolutely nothing, however strange, inconsistent, or evil it may seem to us, happens without God's specific consent.

One lady wrote me her amazing story illustrating that point.

She had been born with only one hand, and from the time she was old enough to realize that she was different from other children, she had worn a scarf or a stole over the stump of her arm to hide her handicap. She was always painfully conscious of her deformity, and as a young woman she began to drink to hide her hurt.

She was fifty-six years old at the time she wrote me:

"Six months ago I visited my sister, and she played a tape where you spoke about praising God for every problem or tragedy in your life. As I listened, I felt like someone had hit me in the stomach. I felt sick. After all the years I'd blamed God for my misfortune, I wasn't ready to thank Him for it. I said 'Lord, forget it. I thanked You for freeing me from alcohol, but I can't thank You for this other thing.'

"But no matter how hard I tried, I couldn't get the thought of thanking God off my mind. It bugged me day and night. Finally I said, 'Lord, why don't you get off my back—I'll do anything for you, but not that! I just can't.' Still, I couldn't find any rest. At last I played the tape once more. This time I heard something I'd missed before. You said that when the young soldier and his wife found themselves *unable* to thank God for the terrible thing they were threatened by, they at last said they were *willing to try*. The rest seemed to come easy. About that time, I'd reached the point where I was willing to try almost anything, just to get some rest. So I told God I was *willing* to try, even if I was sure I wasn't *able*. As soon as I'd said it, it seemed like a load of many years just rolled off my shoulders. I started to praise the Lord— my tears flowed—and it was like the song says, 'Heaven came down and glory filled my soul!' In the middle of all this rejoicing, the Lord spoke to me and said, 'Wait a minute; I'm not through with you yet!' I sat up. What possibly more could there be? I'd just made the supreme sacrifice and thanked God for the deformity I'd hated all my life! But very clearly the words formed in my head:

" 'You are not to carry a stole or a scarf over the stump of your hand anymore!'

"I felt an instant tightening-up inside. 'No, Lord,' I muttered. 'That's going too far. Don't ask me to do that.'

" 'As long as you're hiding it, you're not really thankful; you're still ashamed,' came the gentle reproach. Tearfully, I conceded.

" 'I'm willing to try,' I promised. 'But You've got to make me able.'

"The next time I had occasion to leave the house was when I was called for jury duty. I dressed and automatically reached for my stole. Instantly the warning came. 'No. No!'

"I said, 'All right, God, I'll start out without it, but I am not going to promise I won't come back for it!'

"For the first time in my life I stepped outside the front door without the protective covering to hide my missing hand. As soon as I closed the door behind me, all embarrassment, the shame, and the sense of guilt were washed away! I knew for the first time in my life what it was like to be really free. I knew that God loves me just as I am. Praise the Lord!"

God permits every circumstance of our life for a good reason. Through it, He intends to bring about His perfect and loving plan for us. God permitted that lady to be born without a hand because He loves her. God permitted Satan to harass Job because He loved Job. God permitted Christ to hang on the cross because He loved His Son, and He loved us. God allowed the darkness and evil forces of this world to gain an *apparent* victory—apparent to our senses—yet all the while God's perfect plan for the salvation of the world was being worked out.

No one knew this better than Jesus. Some readers have written me, stating that Jesus complained when He hung on the cross and cried out, "My God, My God, why hast thou forsaken me?"

But to think that Jesus complained is in complete contradiction with everything Jesus said and did about His crucifixion.

No one knew better than Jesus every detail of God's plan to save the world. Jesus had often told his disciples about His coming crucifixion and resurrection, and He had quoted for them passages from the Psalms and Prophets foretelling His sacrifice on the cross. Jesus even urged His disciples to rejoice over what was to happen.

"Remember what I told you," He said. "I am going away, but I will come back to you again. If you really love me, you will be very happy for me, for now I can go to the Father, who is greater than I am" (John 14:28).

He had also told them that no one could take His life without His consent.

"The Father loves me because I lay down my life that I may have it back again. No one can kill me without my consent—I lay down my life voluntarily. For I have the right and power to lay it down when I want to and also the right and power to take it again. For the Father has given me this right" (John 10:17-18).

110

The disciples had been told the real truth, but when the going got rough, they reacted to the apparent victory of evil and rushed to defend Jesus against the soldiers who came to arrest Him.

Jesus stopped them. "Put away your sword," He said. "Don't you realize that I could ask my Father for thousands of angels to protect us, and he would send them instantly? But if I did, how would the Scriptures be fulfilled that describe what is happening now?" (Matt. 26:52-54).

Jesus knew that God's Word, the Scriptures, must be fulfilled. *No* circumstances or action on our part can change the final outworking of God's Word. Jesus Himself was subject to the Word, although He *is* the Word become flesh.

The Jews who surrounded the cross where Jesus hung were familiar with the passages in the Old Testament foretelling the coming of their Messiah who would be crucified for their sins.

The words Jesus cried out, "My God, my God, why hast thou forsaken me?" were the introductory words to the well-known Psalm 22, a psalm of praise and victory, telling of the crucifixion and future reign of the Messiah King.

Jesus' agony on the cross was very real. The nails that pierced His hands hurt Him as much as they would hurt us if we were hanging there. But Jesus knew that his suffering was not a victory for Satan and the forces of evil, but part of God's plan. Jesus praised God *for* the suffering, because He knew it would bring the final victory over evil in the world.

"My God, my God, why have You forsaken me?" Jesus cried out, and the Psalm continues, "Why are You so far from helping me, and from the words of my groaning? . . . But You are holy, O You Who dwell in . . . the praises of Israel . . . Our fathers trusted in You; they . . . were confident—and You delivered them . . . But I am . . . the scorn of men, and despised by the people. Everyone who sees me mocks and sneers and shrugs. 'Is this the one who claims the Lord delights in him? We'll believe it when we see God rescue him!' . . . I am surrounded by fearsome enemies, strong as the giant bulls from Bashan. They come at me with open jaws, like roaring lions attacking their prey. My strength has drained away like water, and all my bones are out of joint. My heart melts like wax; my strength has dried up like sun-baked clay; my tongue sticks to my mouth, for you have laid me in the dust of death. The enemy, this gang of evil men, circles me like a pack of dogs; they have pierced my hands and feet. I can count every bone in my body. See these men of evil gloat and stare; they divide my clothes among themselves by a toss of the dice. But be not far from me, O Lord; O my help, hasten to aid me! I will praise you to all my brothers; I will stand up before the congregation and testify of the wonderful things you have done. 'Praise the Lord, each one of you who fears him,' I will say. 'Each of you must fear and reverence his name. Let all Israel sing his praises, for he has not despised my cries of deep despair; he has not turned and walked away. When I cried to him, he heard and came. Yes, I will stand and praise you before all the people. I will publicly fulfill my vows in the presence of all who reverence your name.

"The poor shall eat and be satisfied; all who seek the Lord shall find him and shall praise his name. Their hearts shall rejoice with everlasting joy. The whole earth shall see it and return to the Lord; the people of every nation shall worship him. For the Lord is King and rules the nations. Both proud and humble together, all who are mortal—born to die—shall worship him. Posterity shall serve him; they shall tell of the Lord to the next generation. They shall come and shall declare His righteousness to a people yet to be born, that He has done it" (*Living Bible* and *Amplified Bible*).

The Amplified Bible adds to the last line, "It is finished!" the last words Jesus breathed before He gave up His spirit and died (John 19:30).

Jesus had often referred to the prophet Isaiah who foretold with amazing accuracy His life and death and future reign.

"But He was wounded and bruised for *our* sins. He was chastised that we might have peace; he was lashed—and we were healed! We are the ones who strayed away like sheep! We, who left God's paths to follow our own. Yet God laid on him the guilt and sins of every one of us! He was oppressed and he was afflicted, yet he never said a word. He was brought as a lamb to the slaughter; and as a sheep before her shearers is dumb, so he stood silent before the ones condemning him. From prison and trial they led him away to his death. But who among the people of that day realized it was their sins that he was dying for—that he was suffering their punishment? He was buried like a criminal in a rich man's grave; but he had done no wrong, and had never spoken an evil word.

"Yet it was the Lord's good plan to bruise him and fill him with grief. But when his soul has been made an offering for sin, then he shall have a multitude of children, many heirs. He shall live again and God's program shall prosper in his hands. And when he sees all that is accomplished by the anguish of his soul, he shall be satisfied; and because of what he has experienced, my righteous Servant shall make many to be counted righteous before God, for he shall bear all their sins. Therefore I will give him the honors of one who is mighty and great, because he has poured out his soul unto death. He was counted as a sinner, and he bore the sins of many, and he pled with God for sinners" (Isa. 53:5-12).

Jesus knew that His crucifixion was not a thwarting of God's plan, but a fulfillment of it. The disciples, however, didn't understand. They saw the crucifixion of Jesus as an end to all their hopes and dreams for the future. They didn't remember Jesus' words when He had told them, "You have sorrow now, but I will see you again and then you will rejoice and no one can rob you of that joy" (John 16:22).

The disciples weren't looking forward to seeing Jesus again, and when they were told that He was no longer in the tomb, they thought His body had been stolen.

Later that day, two of Jesus' followers walked along the road from Jerusalem to Emmaus. They were talking about Jesus' death when suddenly Jesus Himself came and walked beside them. But they didn't recognize Him.

He looked at their sad faces and said, "What are you so concerned about?"

"Haven't you heard?" one of them named Cleopas said. "You must be the only person in Jerusalem who hasn't heard about the terrible things that happened there last week."

Jesus listened as they poured out their sad tale to Him, about the wonderful Jesus of Nazareth who had done such great miracles that they were sure He was the Messiah who had come to rescue Israel, but the religious leaders had handed Him over to the Roman government and He had been crucified. The men spoke as if they had just witnessed the greatest tragedy the world had ever known. On top of it all, they said, the body of Jesus was missing from the tomb, and some women said they'd seen angels who told them that Jesus was alive. The men seemed certain that the last bit of news could only be a fairy tale.

"Then Jesus said to them, 'You are such foolish, foolish people! You find it so hard to believe all that the prophets wrote in the Scriptures. Wasn't it clearly predicted by the prophets that the Messiah would have to suffer all these things before entering his time of glory?'

"Then Jesus quoted them passage after passage from the writings of the prophets, beginning with the book of Genesis and going right on through the Scriptures, explaining what the passages meant and what they said about himself" (Luke 24:25-27).

By this time they were coming near Emmaus, and since it was getting late, the two men asked the stranger to spend the night with them. They still hadn't recognized Him!

Jesus came home with them, and when "they sat down to eat, he asked God's blessing on the food and then took a small loaf of bread and broke it and was passing it over to them, when suddenly—it was as though their eyes were opened—they recognized him!" (Luke 24:30-31).

At last they believed. But for so long they had been able to see only the outward circumstances and had completely missed seeing God's perfect plan unfolding.

The disciples had seen their leader crucified, an apparent triumph of evil over good, and they had taken it as proof that God was *not* present with them. Yet, had they believed God's Word spoken through the prophets, they would have taken the same circumstances as evidence that God *was* with them and working out His plan.

We, too, are like the disciples. When trials and sorrows come our way, our first reaction is, "Oh God, why have you forsaken me?"

But Jesus said, "Here on earth you *will* have many trials and sorrows; but cheer up, for I have overcome the world" (John 16:33).

If we truly believed the words of Jesus, we'd see our circumstances as evidence of God's presence with us, and we'd praise and thank Him for them, instead of complaining and grumbling.

We shake our head at the world conditions and say, "Now *there* is plenty of evidence that God isn't doing much these days."

But Jesus told his followers to expect wars, earthquakes, famines, insurrections, epidemics, pollution, sexual revolution, and so on down the list—a perfect picture of the world we live in, and a promise that it would be getting worse.

Jesus said, "Now when these things begin to take place, look up and raise your heads, because your redemption is drawing near!" (Luke 21:28 RSV).

When things get worse in this world of ours, it is no evidence that God is absent or indifferent. Quite the contrary. All these signs are evidence that God is very near, that every part of His plan and purpose is being fulfilled, just as His Word has promised us.

Jesus told His disciples to rejoice with Him over His crucifixion. Had they been able to trust in His word, they could have experienced joy instead of grief. God's Word tells us to rejoice in our trials.

Peter wrote, "Trust [ing in Jesus] . . . even now you are happy with the inexpressible joy that comes from heaven itself" (I Pet. 1:8).

So what will you believe? Will you walk along your road as did the two men going toward Emmaus, saddened and preoccupied by the outward circumstances, convinced that God is far away? Or will you let your eyes be opened and be thankful?

Receive the bread, the Word, the life, the peace, the joy that Jesus is offering you. See that Jesus is with you, and that God is working in every circumstance of your life to meet your need.

The very thing you think is a painful proof of God's absence from your life is in fact His loving provision to draw you toward Himself—so that you joy may be full!

Look up and praise Him! He loves you, and He dwells in the praises of His people!

LET ALL THE JOYS OF THE GODLY WELL UP IN PRAISE TO THE LORD, for it is right to praise him!

Play joyous melodies of praise upon the lyre and on the harp!

Compose new songs of praise to him, accompanied skillfully on the harp; sing joyfully.

For all God's words are right, and everything he does is worthy of our trust.

He loves whatever is just and good; the earth is filled with his tender love.

He merely spoke, and the heavens were formed, and all the galaxies of stars.

He made the oceans, pouring them into his vast reservoirs.

Let everyone in all the world—men, women and children—fear the Lord and stand in awe of him.

For when he but spoke, the world began! It appeared at his command!

And with a breath he can scatter the plans of all the nations who oppose him, but His own plan stands forever. His intentions are the same for every generation.

Blessed is the nation whose God is the Lord, whose people he has chosen as his own.

The Lord gazes down upon mankind from heaven where he lives. He has made their hearts and closely watches everything they do.

The best-equipped army cannot save a king—for great strength is not enough to save anyone. A war horse is a poor risk for winning victories—it is strong but it cannot save.

But the eyes of the Lord are watching over those who fear him, who rely upon his steady love.

He will keep them from death even in time of famine!

We depend upon the Lord alone to save us. Only he can help us; he protects us like a shield.

No wonder we are happy in the Lord! For we are trusting him! We trust his holy name.

Yes, Lord, let your constant love surround us, for our hopes are in you alone.

—Psalm 33

115

Publishers note:

Comments, inquiries, and requests for speaking engagements should be directed to:

Merlin Carothers
Box 2085
Escondido, CA 92025

TA11 DAVID duPLESSIS, Author of "THE SPIRIT BADE ME GO"

TA12 WENDELL WALLACE, Author of "BORN TO BURN"

TA13 DR. HOWARD ERVIN, Author of "THESE ARE NOT DRUNKEN"

TA14 CLINTON WHITE, Author of "FROM THE BELLY OF THE WHALE"

TA15 DR. ROBERT FROST, Author of "AGLOW WITH THE SPIRIT"

TA16 DR. J. RODMAN WILLIAMS, Author of "THE ERA OF THE SPIRIT"

TA17 SONNY ARGUINZONI, Author of "GOD'S JUNKIE"

TA18 KATHRYN KUHLMAN — "AN HOUR WITH KATHRYN KUHLMAN"

TA19 KEVIN RANAGHAN, Author of "CATHOLIC PENTE-COSTALS"

TA20 CHARLES SIMPSON — "A SOUTHERN BAPTIST LOOKS AT PENTECOST"

TA21 WILLARD CANTELON — "THE NEW WORLD MONEY SYSTEM"

TA22 THE CHARISMATIC RENEWAL—Bredesen, Ervin, Evans, Brown, Roberts

TA23 FR. JOSEPH ORSINI, Author of "HEAR MY CONFESSION"

TA24 PHIL SAINT, Author of "AMAZING SAINTS"

TA25 PAT ROBERTSON, Author of "SHOUT IT FROM THE HOUSETOPS"

TA26 MALCOLM SMITH, Author of "TURN YOUR BACK ON THE PROBLEM"

TA27 FRANK FOGLIO, Author of "HEY, GOD!"

RECORDS — $4.95

MS120 AN HOUR WITH KATHRYN KUHLMAN

M7 NICKY CRUZ — 7" record

M13-72 NICKY CRUZ — 12" record

M125 NEW WORLD MONEY SYSTEM — Willard Cantelon

SUGGESTED INEXPENSIVE PAPERBACK BOOKS
WHEREVER PAPERBACKS ARE SOLD
OR USE ORDER FORM.

A NEW SONG—Boone	AA3	$ .95
AGLOW WITH THE SPIRIT—Frost	L326	.95
AMAZING SAINTS—Saint	L409	2.50
AND FORBID NOT TO SPEAK—Ervin	L329	.95
AND SIGNS FOLLOWED—Price	P002	1.50
ANGLES OF LIGHT?—Freeman	A506	.95
ANSWERS TO PRAISE—Carothers	L670	1.95
ARMSTRONG ERROR—DeLoach	L317	.95
AS AT THE BEGINNING—Harper	L721	1.95
BAPTISM IN THE SPIRIT—Schep	L343	1.50
BAPTISM IN THE SPIRIT—BIBLICAL —Cockburn	16F	.65
BAPTISM OF FIRE—Harper	8F	.60
BAPTIZED IN ONE SPIRIT—Baker	1F	.60
BAPTIZED IN THE SPIRIT—Clark	P9	.75
BEN ISRAEL—Katz	A309	.75
BLACK TRACKS—Miles	A298	.95
BORN TO BURN—Wallace	A508	.95
CATHOLIC PENTECOSTALISM—McDonnell	P6	.60
CHALLENGING COUNTERFEIT—Gasson	L102	.95
COMING ALIVE—Buckingham	A501	.95
CONFESSIONS OF A HERETIC—Hunt	L31X	2.50
COUNSELOR TO COUNSELOR—Campbell	L335	1.50
CRISIS AMERICA—Otis	AA1	.95
DAYSPRING—White	L334	1.95
DISCOVERY (Booklet)—Frost	F71	.50
ERA OF THE SPIRIT—Williams	L322	1.95
15 STEPS OUT—Mumford	L106	1.50
FROM THE BELLY OF THE WHALE—White	A318	.95
GATHERED FOR POWER—Pulkinghm	AA4	2.50
GOD BREAKS IN—Congdon	L313	1.95

PIONEERS OF REVIVAL—Clarke	L723	.95
POWER IN PRAISE—Carothers	L342	1.95
POWER FOR THE BODY—Harper	4F	.85
PRAYER MEETINGS—Cavnar	P2	.50
PREACHER WITH A BILLY CLUB—Asmuth	A209	.95
PRISON TO PRAISE—Carothers	A504	.95
PROPHECY A GIFT FOR THE BODY	2F	.65
PSEUDO CHRISTIANS—Jarman	A516	.95
REAL FAITH—Price	P000	1.50
RUN BABY RUN—Cruz	L101	.95
RUN BABY RUN—Cruz (Comic Book)		.20
SATAN SELLERS—Warnke	L794	2.50
SOUL PATROL—Bartlett	A500	.95
SPEAKING WITH GOD—Cantelon	L336	.95
SPIRIT BADE ME GO—DuPlessis	L325	.95
SPIRITUAL AND PHYSICAL HEALING —Price	P003	1.95
SPIRITUAL GIFTS—Clark	P3	.50
SPIRITUAL WARFARE—Harper	A505	.95
STRONGER THAN PRISON WALLS —Wurmbrand	A956	.95
TAKE ANOTHER LOOK—Mumford	L338	2.50
THERE'S MORE—Hall	L344	1.50
THESE ARE NOT DRUNKEN—Ervin	L105	2.50
THIS EARTH'S END—Benson	A513	.95
THIS WHICH YE SEE AND HEAR—Ervin	L728	1.95
TONGUES UNDER FIRE—Lillie	3F	.85
TURN YOUR BACK ON THE PROBLEM —Smith	L034	1.95
TWO WORLDS—Price	P004	1.95
UNDERGROUND SAINTS—Wurmbrand	U-1	.95
WALK IN THE SPIRIT—Harper	L319	.95
WE'VE BEEN ROBBED—Meloon	L339	1.50
YOU CAN KNOW GOD—Price	P005	.75
YOUR NEW LOOK—Buckingham	A503	.95

FINALLY!!! A COMPLETE ALL-PURPOSE—APPROVED—STUDY BIBLE !!!

THE LOGOS INTERNATIONAL STUDY BIBLE

OLD AND NEW TESTAMENT: AMERICAN STANDARD VERSION
The world's finest Topical Analysis prepared by renowned scholars

WITH:--AMERICAN STANDARD TEXT (The Rock of Biblical Integrity)
THE OLD AND NEW TESTAMENT
VARIORUM RENDERINGS★ 150 scholars offer special helps, suggested word translations, meanings.
TOPICAL ANALYSIS—A complete Bible analysis in one volume.
CROSS-REFERENCES—100,000 cross-references.
INDEX, CONCORDANCE
MAPS

IN ADDITION:—THE LOGOS LAYMAN'S COMMENTARY ON THE HOLY SPIRIT
With special reference index on every verse in the New Testament referring to the Holy Spirit.

COMMENTARY EDITOR: **JOHN REA, Th.D.**—Biblical Research Editor

CONTRIBUTING EDITORS: **HOWARD ERVIN, Th.D.**
RAY CORVIN, D.R.E., Ph.D.
ERWIN PRANGE, B.D.,Th.M.
DAVID du PLESSIS, D.D.
J. RODMAN WILLIAMS, Ph.D.
Fr. JOSEPH ORSINI, Ed.D.

FREE CATALOG
at religious bookstores
or
LOGOS BIBLE
185 North Avenue
Plainfield, NJ 07060

Realizing the need for a quality but easily 'understandable HOLY SPIRIT COMMENTARY, the editors combined their efforts in supplying a verse-by-verse analysis of the New Testament.

★Variorum renderings are alternate suggested words and phrases taken from ancient manuscripts and offered as alternatives by leading Bible scholars. Ancient Bible texts, their meanings, origin, and scholars' opinions are included.

Church in the Home

FREE
SAMPLE COPY
OF

LOGOS

An International Charismatic Journal

Worldwide Coverage
Feature Articles
Book Reviews
Trends